PIKE

The Predator becomes the Prey

PIKE

The Predator becomes the Prey

JOHN BAILEY
and
MARTYN PAGE

The Crowood Press

First published in 1985 by
THE CROWOOD PRESS
Crowood House, Ramsbury
Marlborough, Wiltshire SN8 2HE

© John Bailey and Martyn Page

British Library Cataloguing in Publication Data

Bailey, John
Pike: the predator becomes the prey.
1. Pike fishing
I. Title   II. Page, Martyn
799.1′753   SH691.P6

ISBN 0-946284-47-4

Typeset by Quadraset Ltd, Midsomer Norton, Avon
Printed in Great Britain by Robert Hartnoll Ltd, Bodmin

To Sharon, Lynne and pike everywhere!

CONTENTS

Acknowledgements   1
Foreword   3
Preface   5
Our Stories   7
Getting to Grips with Larger Pike   17
Advanced Developments in Methods and Techniques   23

THE FENS   31
Two Inventive Pikers   33
One Way with Fenland Pike   39
LOCHS AND LOUGHS   47
Lomond and the Lochs of Scotland   48
An Approach to Irish Loughs   64
Trolling English Style   75
RIVER PIKE   77
Big River Piking   79
Piking on the Wessex Rivers   90
A New River Waveney Record   99
LARGE STILLWATERS   103
The Drifting Technique   105
Reservoirs, Gravel Pits and Large Lakes   117
Jack Livebaits   135
NORFOLK BROADLANDS   139
Broadland Piking   144
The Challenge of Broadland   152
A Modern Broadland Master   160
Always Broadland Masters   164

The Final Meeting   169
Authors and Contributors   175

ACKNOWLEDGEMENTS

We wish to thank all contributors, especially our artist Chris Turnbull, and helpful pike men everywhere. Thanks also to Janet and Ann for help with secretarial work, and to Paul Billing for the use of his word processor.

In addition, we are grateful to the following people for use of the photographs indicated below:

Mick Brown: pages 80, 81, 83, 87; colour plates 17, 18, 24
Gord Burton: pages 50, 51, 55, 57, 60, 62; colour plates 10, 14
Jan Eggers: pages 66, 67
Neville Fickling: page 70
Vic Gibson: page 107
Steve Harper: colour plate 26
Tony Lovell: pages 34, 114, 125 (both), 126, 127 (both), 128;
   colour plates 3, 4, 5, 6, 7
Tony Miles: pages 93, 141
Keith Mottram: page 41
Bob Mousley: pages 91, 97, 98; colour plates 16, 22, 23
Dave Plummer: page 157; colour plate 29
Roy Smyth: pages 64, 69, 71, 73
Joe Taylor: colour plate 9
Eddie Turner: pages 109, 111; colour plate 21
John Watson: pages 32, 35, 37, 44, 45, 53, 61, 133;
   colour plates 2, 8, 25

FOREWORD

I was rather surprised when Martyn Page asked me if I was interested in writing the foreword to a pike book he and John Bailey were compiling. Why on earth ask a Dutchman who doesn't know the contributors to the book, who has hardly fished for pike in England and to whom several of the methods described look like witchcraft? All kinds of questions came bubbling up in my pike-disturbed mind. Is the book so bad that no Englishman will associate himself with it? Do English anglers believe all my fairy tales about big pike and catfish from the Continent, and is this a way to persuade them to buy a new fairy tale? Or might it be that a foreword by the President of the Dutch-Belgium Pike Anglers' Club will give this book international status?

Plenty of questions, so I phoned Martyn and said that I was interested but first I wanted to read the typescript. A few days later I started to read a few hundred unillustrated loose pages. I had told Martyn that I would not do the foreword if I did not like the book, but after a few chapters I phoned him and agreed to do it.

This 'Pike Ferret' (a nickname Fred Buller has given me) consumed the pages like a hungry pike swallows a fat livebait, but then another question arose — what should I write in the foreword? Viewing this book with the eyes of a foreign pike fisherman, I decided not to go on about how I would have liked more information on lure fishing and how to use a depth-finder, or that I would have used one size smaller hook on a particular rig. No, I asked myself time and time again what value has this book for the international

pike fishing fraternity, and the answer is — a lot! The book is written by a group of *pike fishermen*, not writers who fish now and then, so it deals with practical bankside techniques, telling pike fishermen all over the world how to tackle different waters under different circumstances.

Fishing is becoming more and more international. People in the USA have become interested in European methods of live and deadbaiting, English specialist anglers travel over Europe to tell their colleagues about their methods, and pike angler clubs now pool their knowledge, regardless of whether they are concerned with pike in Minnesota, Norfolk or Amsterdam. Increasingly pike are becoming the number one sport fish in many countries — quite a change from thirty years ago — and consequently more people are studying pike behaviour. There is a great deal in this book about variations in the behaviour of pike found in different waters — an aspect which makes the book so interesting. The contributors try to understand why pike do this or that during certain periods and they try to adapt their way of fishing for given circumstances, as no one method of fishing covers the whole pike fishing season.

Adapt yourself, this is the key to success, and many times you will read how trying a new approach has caught a sought-after fish. This book teaches that pike in different types of water have their own personality, and to catch them you have to vary your approach according to the environment, whether it be the Broads, lochs, reservoirs or rivers. As I see it this book tells us once again that the more we learn about pike the more convinced we are how little we know. In my opinion this is what makes the pike such an interesting sport fish, for where would be mystery surrounding pike if it were easy to catch a forty pounder?

Finally, I liked the enthusiasm of the contributors, the way they try to convince the reader that pike fishing can be a valuable contribution to an angler's life; no dull stories here from specialists who list how many twenties and thirties they have managed to catch. No, pike fishing is a great sport no matter if you catch just a few jacks or many doubles in a day's fishing, and we have to maintain it this way.

I hope that this book will bring pike fishermen all over the world the pleasure that I derived from the typescript – not only in reading but in practising its teachings. And although I had to read into the late hours of the night, with my wife urging me to switch off the light and close my eyes, I can only say to the contributors of the book: thank you in the name of the international pike fishing fraternity.

Jan Eggers ('The Pike Ferret')

PREFACE

Once more the small roach swam into the shallow bay, only too aware of the pair of staring eyes fixed upon it. The eyes were unmoving, unblinking, as cold as a death that comes in the winter. The roach sensed the ever increasing danger, and growing fright made its swimming more erratic and hence became more attractive to the brain behind those eyes. The injured, desperate fish was a transmitter of helplessness, and the trigger to furious hunger.

The great huntress felt herself more and more aroused. Instinctively her body wound itself to attack the roach. She had not eaten for a week, not since a moorhen had ventured too close to her lie in the dead sedges. Now, this morsel would keep her satisfied at least overnight. This mouse in her den, so insolent to swim so close, was sealing its own fate.

The dorsal of the pike stiffened, a thrill of menace rippled along the flanks until they quivered taut as a bowstring. The roach knew now and turned away upwards, towards the light. In plumes of spray, the water heaved around it.

Line hissed from the reel. For a second, the fisherman missed his heartbeat. The trap had been sprung. In a few short seconds, the predator had become the prey.

OUR STORIES

We have decided to begin this book with tales about two wicked pike, fish that mean much to us, for many different reasons and they are both signposts to the way in which successful big pike men work.

John Bailey's story

I have a great belief in this book. I am confident that Martyn and I have assembled some of the best advice ever given in this sport of ours, and, at this moment I am beholden to the teaching of others. You see, a short while back, I caught my biggest pike and many of the ideas that led to its downfall came from other anglers. It so happens that all of them are contributing to this book. So we have come a full circle. This is the story.

Late in 1984, I was allowed to fish a trout water for pike, the lake only opened for coarse fishing for a few days each year. Of course, I was excited at the prospect, for any study of the history of big pike shows that they thrive in large waters, where there is a trout population and where they are the species neglected by anglers. I knew that for a short while I would at least be close to immense fish.

From here on, though, I faced problems. The fact that I had only four days on the water meant that I had to make the most of my time there. Whatever methods and bait I decided to use had to give me as great a chance as possible, or else I would regret it and probably remain fishless.

Locating a pike would be my most difficult task. The idea haunted me. The pit is not massive, but over twenty acres, and a wild place in the winter with bottom con-

tours like the face of some meteor-blasted planet. I could not get a boat out on the water and explore it with an echo sounder or plumb-line for drop-offs or gullies or any locating feature. And, remember, the water is rarely fished, so there is no tradition of good areas to draw upon, no local expertise or knowledge to help me. Even though I fly-fished the pit in spring and summer, this only taught me something about the margins, nothing about the further uncharted water.

Using rainbow trout for bait was initially suggested by Chris Turnbull, our artist for this book. Trout almost certainly form a large part of the pike's food here, and in the short period ahead of me, I placed a great deal of confidence in using their staple diet. Sea-fish deadbaits very probably had never been seen by the majority of the fish and I feared they might be treated suspiciously as aliens for some time. Time was what I could not afford to lose.

Without the knowledge of hot-spots in the lake or any proven features, I believed it was vital to cover as much water as possible, to get past the margins and search out the unexploited areas. I wanted to get my live trout and deadbaits into the virgin expanses of the pit, to cover as many pike as possible, to fish as positively as I was able to.

One bay in particular attracted me. At its southern end lay the trout cages with several thousand occupants; their activity, and the chance of occasional escapees, I believed would draw pike into the region. Also, during the dry summer of 1984, when levels were low in the pit, I had seen that there was a large plateau in the middle

John Bailey, dressed against the cold, displays a 21lb fish.

of this bay, with a network of deeper troughs across it, and promising drop-offs surrounding it. This area began approximately eighty to a hundred yards from the bank and was about an acre in extent. Whilst it would be possible to cast frozen deadbaits to the lip of the plateau, I wanted to do more than this. I needed to search the area, and to present a live bait delicately, which no eighty yard cast would allow me to do.

I knew that progress had been made on large stillwaters by some of the London area anglers in particular and that one of them, Eddy Turner, had started to market specialised tackle for the job of drifting baits long distances, far beyond the ranges I had fished before. I phoned Dave Plummer who I knew had used drifting tackle before and could provide me with the information and the floats that I needed. A fifteen minute call and I had at least grasped the basics of the method. Another contributor to the book, Roger Miller, collected my new floats, line and greases, and even delivered some trout to my door as bait. It seemed then, that I had a plan and the means to put it into practice.

On Sunday, 23 December 1984, I was on the lake an hour before the deliciously mild dawn broke. There was drizzle in the air and a moderate wind chased the heavy clouds low over the surrounding hills. Not only was the wind force perfect but it came from the south-west, the exact quarter I had hoped for. From the point where I stood, I could now drift a bait before me a hundred yards to the drop-off, further still over the plateau and across the gullies and troughs that I knew had never been fished before.

As it became light, I began my first drift, the great orange sail float showing well in the gloom. It was set at seven feet and below it worked a six ounce rainbow trout. The float caught the wind and within ten minutes or so I had reached the plateau. I was over depth. The float dragged then dived down. I began the long reel and re-adjusted the float to five feet. On the next drift, I found the bait just skirted the bottom working all the while.

I explored the edges of the plateau. The morning wore on. Heavier rain began to fall and the promise and expectancy of the dawn began to ebb away. Jack, the fishery manager, called from the club house and I had half a mind to give into him and take a cup of tea before the fire.

I decided first to put one last drift across

the very middle of the plateau, to let the wind take my bait clear to the far side if need be, a distance well over two hundred yards. The float showed up well around a hundred yards away, and I knew my bait was over the shallows, covering troughs as it went. Every five yards I checked the float to make the bait work either side of its drift line, and, when I had covered this wider area, I let it go again, sailing before the wind.

Success or no, I was enjoying myself. It was as though I were trotting a river for roach, only on a massive scale, at a huge distance, with gear strong enough to land the predator rather than just the prey. I felt

An indication of the pike's impressive length and huge girth. This fish is typical of fast growing, trout feeding pike which have relatively small heads and bulky bodies.

the master of the pit, as at 120 yards my float danced at my command.

A little after 10 a.m., at this extreme range, the float, that great neon sail disappeared. Its going was so quick, so complete, that in that grey light I felt unsure, almost unnerved. I told myself that the bait had snagged again, that I was on to uncharted water and that the plateau had shallowed up into a ridge. But deep down, I knew that this was not so, rather that my drift had located a pike at last.

I wound tight, ironing out the loops and meanders in the hundred plus yards of line. I felt the tension grow. I was direct to the fish. Then I moved back from the water, the rod arching over my left shoulder. It stayed there, hooked over and held in a half circle. Nothing moved, doubts crept in. A snag still seemed more than possible.

I am wary of describing battles with fish. They can easily become tedious episodes of

unstoppable runs as the angler heroically counters all. Now, I will only say that when that pike moved, it was with a power I had never dreamed of. For over twenty minutes its will was irresistible, and in the soft English countryside to be attached to such a creature was awesome. When I saw the pike at the last, a light mottled green in a swirl of angry water, it looked like the dragon of our myths and legends.

At the bankside I had to be a hero, a junior St George. The mesh of the landing net began to tear with the weight of the pike's white and cream belly, and I leaped in and cradled the giant on to the land. The fish weighed thirty-six pounds four ounces. She was a savage, still noble and dignified in defeat. The hooks had fallen from her jaw as she hit the net, and all I needed to do was admire and return her. She was not my triumph alone. She was an object lesson in angling education, in taking advice from master fishermen.

Martyn Page's story

January 1981, and a new year dawned with hope of new fortunes. Luck, that final ingredient so essential for success, had been completely absent during the course of the previous year's pike fishing. True, I had caught a large number of pike, in fact I had ceased counting at over 150 since October 1980, but their size was disappointing. I doubt whether I'd ever seen so many seven pound pike, and wherever the doubles and twenties were it was certain they were not gracing my landing net!

But perhaps I should have expected this. Remember this was in the early days of the Norfolk pike resurgence. Between 1982 and 1985 there has been a spate of large pike from the area, but at the beginning of the 1980s to hear of, let alone catch, a fish

Opposite John Bailey is staggered by his 36lb 4oz lake pike.

of twenty-five pounds or above was extremely rare. Indeed big twenty and thirty pound fish could be counted each year on one hand. In short we knew that our success could not be guaranteed.

I was part of a team, the four of us fishing with the single objective of catching very large pike. Our waters contained an abundance of jack, but we also hoped for a few of those rare heavyweights. Unexpected success heralded the early days when Dave Humphries landed a huge fast water pike from the River Waveney and at an ounce over thirty pounds we hoped the scene was set for the capture of several more. A year later though, we had encountered only one other really large fish, and that had come adrift during the fight.

It was in the third week of January that our luck began to change when, as eagle-eyed as ever, Steve Harper noticed a small news report of several fish from one of the waters we had marked as 'possibles'. This broad was an old favourite of mine, and had produced fish of over twenty pounds for us in the past. Mystery, nostalgia, call it what you will, surrounded the water, for one day, whilst playing a fourteen pound pike, a fish over twice the size chased my captive to within yards of the boat. The pursuit was short and, as the larger fish retreated to the depths, I frantically placed baits all around. But this was to no avail. The mists and the dusk settled over him for that evening.

Our enthusiasm for the broad was now rekindled by this news report, for although it contained no monsters there had been a large catch of fish, and this was of interest. It had been almost unknown to catch many pike from this heartache water, and we considered an average of one pike per session an achievement. A catch of a dozen fish, as the report suggested, was outstanding. Could it be that the fish had come from the adjacent river and on to the broad early this year in the mild weather, with spawning already in mind? More essentially, would any of the enormous females be with them?

The team decided that in order not to place too much hope or effort in this one water Steve Harper and John Watson would pay a visit there, whilst Dave Humphries and myself went searching on another target water, the Thurne. Our day proved uneventful. The Thurne produced only seven pound fish, consistent with our earlier visits there. Even if our hunch for the Thurne was to come true in a very big way later, it would not do so for us that season. That same day Steve and John's results on our refound broad a few miles away, were sufficient to ensure that it remained the centre of attention for the rest of that winter.

The fish had been found almost immediately in shallow water at the broad entrance, so it did seem that the pike were moving off the river. The day had ended with a number of fish to twenty-three pounds. Of course the next weekend saw the entire team of four keen anglers fishing there very hard, and eventually I was rewarded when a screaming run produced, not another seven pound pike, but a fish some four pounds heavier. Perhaps the tide on 1981 was beginning to turn. At that stage, however, the weather decided to play a part, as temperatures plummeted for the rest of the day with no sport forthcoming. All too soon the broad had returned to its usual self – one hard struggle.

Conditions got no better, but we fished on several times during those following weeks as we felt that success was only a question of time and, perhaps, an improvement in the weather. For John Watson, a member of our team, this proved to be the case. During one bleak day early in February his persistence and perpetual enthusiasm paid a dividend. Throughout the daylight hours only one small pike fell to his rods but then, as in the story books, in

pitch blackness, with the decision to call it a day, with one mighty explosion, an enormous pike took his bait.

Suddenly life had developed added excitement. During the course of that evening, in a quiet smoky corner of the bar, plots and plans were made, theories created, rejected and confirmed. By the end of that evening we were ready to surprise the angling world with success upon success. The next day we all failed!

By mid-February the broad had yielded very few more fish, none of which were large. For many days the water temperature had hovered around freezing and at times half the broad had been covered with a thin layer of ice. Our evening discussions had convinced us that as this was not a heavily fished water, bait was not a problem and the pike were unlikely to be cautious. We were also agreed that the extreme water clarity suggested the use of live as opposed to dead bait. I also felt privately that the cold weather had persisted for so many days now, that hunger must have activated at least some of the fish.

It was in the course of one such evening that realisation dawned. We had become guilty of that most cardinal sin in angling, of shuttered vision. We had spent far too long resting on patchy success in an area which we had decided wrongly was a hotspot. It is often all too easy to convince oneself that an area is 'hot' merely because a few fish have come from it, without analysing the reasons why. In this case the reasons of course were that the fish were moving through that spot after leaving the river, and with the onset of cold weather, possibly they had all left quickly for another area of the broad. It was necessary to return to team-work in order to re-locate these fish.

We decided that we would start next morning with one boat fishing the entrance area and the other searching the

Above *Martyn Page displays a slender 23lb pike that was caught at night and carefully sacked until this early morning picture could be taken.*

Below *John Watson returns a fine Bure twenty.*

deeper water. Dave and I unfortunately drew the short straw, and first light found us in the old area, fast losing our faith. Within two hours I had decided that this was definitely not a hot-spot, more likely it was stone cold. Indeed, I was totally unsettled that morning, convinced that there wasn't a pike within a hundred yards of the bait. As the morning passed the feeling, or a calling, for the deeper water on the far side of the broad grew steadily stronger. I was sure that sometime that day the fish had to feed, and Dave took no convincing when I told him of my convictions and suggested a move. Several years fishing has taught us both that if we experience a strong feeling to change swim or even water, then such feelings should be acted upon. This has been proved to us so many times in the past.

As we rowed across the broad a quick call to John and Steve told us that they too had failed to locate any feeding fish. They had already, during the course of the morning, covered several swims in the deep water by moving regularly and by fishing from separate boats, but there was the one area upon which my attention was fixed that had not been tried. This was the very spot where those few years earlier the fourteen pounder had been chased by that monster out of the evening.

We had soon anchored and cast a selection of paternostered livebaits and static deadbaits around the boat. An hour passed and soon only crumbs were left in the sandwich box and the last dregs of the flask had been emptied. Our sense of optimism had, however, not diminished but strangely had grown. The sense of déjà vu was strong, as if I were being given a second chance at a past opportunity missed. Again memories of that bygone day flowed back. That day too had been very still with a mild dampness in the air, with the whisper that perhaps winter was now passing and warmer weather was on its way. As my

thoughts drifted back I recalled yet again a fleeting glimpse of that big fish, the ivory of its flanks in the gloom, and the bow wave that rocked the boat as it turned away from me. Memories faded rapidly. The past was forgotten as Dave and myself had instantaneous takes, and, as if a switch had been turned on, the pike fed ravenously.

Both those first two fish were about nine pounds, as were the three or four more which followed in quick succession during this feeding spell. All the pike were having livebaits and, in order to take maximum advantage of the situation while it lasted, I quickly switched all my rods to the going method. Even as I changed rigs another two fish were landed, again of around the same size. Eventually retackled, the converted rod was cast slightly away from the main feeding area. I was hoping that possibly a bigger fish was waiting on the edge, reluctant to enter the centre of disturbance. The small roach was taken almost as it hit the water, but the strike failed to connect. I quickly recast. Again a wait of only seconds lay before me before the next run and then, for only the first time that year, I struck straight into a heavyweight pike. I would like to say the fight was spectacular but, typical of winter broads fish, this was not the case. Yet the first sighting of that fish left absolutely no doubt in our minds that at last it had all come together and that this fish represented an ambition achieved.

I still hold childhood memories of my first pike – a fish of one pound nine ounces – and I shall never forget the first twenty pounder, but the fish now lying in the net, an ounce under twenty-nine pounds, will always hold the most cherished place in my mind. It was the epitome of a large broadland pike. A magnificent fish, it had cer-

Opposite *The culmination of a dream for Martyn Page. At 28lb 15oz this remains his largest, most cherished fish.*

tainly never been caught before. With that fish, the blanks were immediately forgotten, the heartbreaks had gone leaving only the euphoria of achievement and success.

And then, if that were not enough, Steve Harper called from his boat close to us. He was into a fish which, despite considerable pressure, had refused to yield after one seemingly infinite run. We had stumbled into one of those Broadland fantasies when all the monsters had come out to feed at once.

With Steve's twenty-two pound pike, came the end of the feeding spell, not only for that day but also for the remainder of the season.

If there are any lessons to be learned from my story, they must be that, having traced the water holding the calibre of fish you desire, you must still find the pike, use the correct bait for the day, and hope to the end that luck plays its part and fortune smiles kindly on you.

GETTING TO GRIPS WITH LARGER PIKE

We intend here to provide an outline of the general approach which has been used successfully many times in the quest for large pike. We will concentrate on the way in which waters holding good pike can be found, and then we will outline how to tackle such a venue. Let us make it clear these are the basics only. The subsequent sections of the book explore piking in greater depth, and our experts pinpoint problems and solutions in far more detail.

Analytical approach

The successful piker makes several conscious decisions. He will decide what size of pike he is after, and how much time, effort and cost he is prepared to sacrifice to his hunt. He will be quite ruthless in his approach, discarding local waters with little potential and looking at more distant ones which will demand more from him in terms of commitment. He will decide how many full days a week he can have on chosen waters, and make sure that he will be there whenever his job allows.

All these factors are for you to decide, but the important message is to draw up a campaign and then stick to it. Good pike are not caught consistently by the uncommitted. Piking is one of the more gruelling branches of the sport and few good ones landed are not worked for.

Locating waters

Equally logical should be the choice of waters to be fished. The initial step is to decide how far you are prepared to travel. The most dedicated pikers, of course, find their radius is confined only by the perimeters within which pike themselves are found. Conversely, the less enthusiastic will fish only the waters on their doorstep. Having decided on the 'travelling perimeter', we would advocate fishing two or three waters with potential. If too many are left on a short list, there is the temptation to switch waters constantly without doing justice to any.

The potential waters will be drawn up by research from maps, local angling guides, bankside visits and conversations with anglers everywhere. Care must be taken with backdated reports, only recent history is important. M.P. knows this through experience. Having obtained permission to fish a water of some sixty acres on which fishing had not been allowed for half a century, he spent a whole morning cutting through alder carr to the entrance dyke, only to find reed encroachment had been rapid. There was less than one acre of open water left, with no pike, or indeed any fish, present.

Very soon a few waters will stand out above the rest. They will fall into one of two groups. These will either be popular waters, producing or having recently produced large pike. Or they will be little fished waters where initial research suggests potential. Let us call these two types of water 'popular' and 'unpiked'.

The pyramid theory

With either popular or unpiked waters, it is important to look carefully at the biological rhythms or cycles of these waters. Here the 'balanced concept' or 'pyramid theory' comes into play. This means that in its natural state a water will only support a specific total weight of pike. All things being equal, the pike population in the water should more or less fall within certain weight bands, with decreasing numbers of pike as their size increases (see diagram below). Effectively, therefore, the result is a pyramid with very few top sized pike. Such a water would probably be an excellent popular fishery with plenty of pike to be caught, but it is unlikely to hold numbers of the type of big pike you might want to catch.

In practice, however, there are many waters where this balance does not exist. Many factors could have upset the pyramid theory: pike culls could have taken place;

pollution or netting operations could have affected the food stocks; large pike could have been removed as glass case trophies; new species of food supply, such as trout, could have been introduced. Any of these events will lead the water to lose its balance which will cause several things to happen. If the food supply is destroyed, any remaining pike will deteriorate in condition, though becoming very easy to catch. In cases where the food remains but many of the pike are removed, at first the survivors should increase their weight as the competition is removed, and for a while a complete weight band could disappear, leaving a water of only jacks and fast growing large fish. J.B.'s thirty-six pound pike came from a water with just such a distorted pyramid.

For the ambitious pikeman, therefore, it will pay to locate waters with an imbalanced pyramid which can sometimes produce monster fish. A good example of imbalance at work is in a typical new gravel

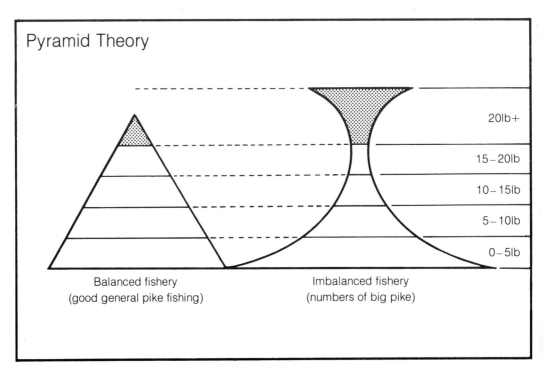

Pyramid Theory

20lb+

15–20lb

10–15lb

5–10lb

0–5lb

Balanced fishery
(good general pike fishing)

Imbalanced fishery
(numbers of big pike)

pit. Often the first fish to find their way into such waters came from an adjacent river. A club stocks the water with large numbers of prey fish and of course those first few pike effectively have a field day. For several years, they grow rapidly without competition, until they breed and a balance is established.

Popular waters

A weekend visit to a popular water will soon give you an idea of the favourite hotspots. Remember though, that if you immediately fish only in these popular swims, you will simply be emulating anglers who have been there before, and probably what was once a hot area has already begun to deteriorate. Secondly, such hot-spots are often created only in the minds of anglers who fish there. One or two pike from an area do not necessarily make it *the* swim. Pike anglers repeatedly fall into the trap of returning to the same old places. We call this 'shuttered' or 'tunnel' vision and every one of us has been guilty of it at some time. Even on popular waters it is important to keep an open mind and go for unfished areas. This means hard work, but it can lead to interesting fishing and previously uncaught pike.

Popular waters require greater thought on baits and rigs. Constant pressure causes a pike to become wary of both live and deadbaits and stereotyped presentation. Pike develop an instinctive knowledge that associates a particular bait with an experience, and on some waters they have switched away from the 'going' bait almost overnight. It is therefore essential to experiment with baits in such a situation, and you will find in the Fenland section a more detailed discussion on this question.

Unpiked waters

Waters where you are alone present a massive challenge, though the rewards can be fantastic. Perhaps the Thurne system presents the best example of the unpiked water.

It was a holiday-maker who made the first significant capture from the system before it became popular, and at that time no one actually believed him. Very few pikemen had been there since the prymnesium outbreak in the 1960s, most being convinced there had been an almost total cull of fish. However, a number of pike survived and their offspring were neglected by anglers. Because of the low number of predators in the water, it seems that their average size was a few pounds greater than their pre-prymnesium ancestors. Norfolk angler, Bill Florey, was one of the first anglers back on the system, which had lain unpiked for many years. In one season he caught fifty pike in excess of twenty pounds.

We would hardly ever consider commencing a campaign on a new unfished water at any time other than October or November. Then the pike are still very active, feeding hard in preparation for a cold weather metabolic slow down. Also the food fish are beginning to form compact shoals and sport can be hectic at times when pike hit into them.

December and January will show a marked slow down in the catch rate, but in February the fish begin to move more once again, perhaps as spawning urges drive them. The first two weeks of March can be excellent, especially if the fish can be found around their spawning grounds. Assuming you start on an unpiked water in the autumn, we would recommend that you fish as a team, with perhaps two or three friends. In this way, confidence and enthusiasm are maintained and it is possible to search more water.

It is important to adopt an analytical approach to location, especially on large waters. A map should be drawn up, and the water can then be grid searched. Swims should be changed regularly, at least every three quarters of an hour if fish are not being caught; in this way a number of fish should be taken quickly, and a picture of the new water, its stocks, and its potential will quickly be built up.

Obvious features should not be ignored during these initial visits. On a trout water, for example, pike will be in residence near the pens, where they expect to find a steady trickle of escapees. Bream patrol routes will also attract pike to lie along them in ambush points. Try not to read the water as a human being, but as a predator considering his prey.

Baits on unpiked waters are no problem whatsoever, and our approach is to use the most easily obtainable bait first. We would begin our campaign with livebaits and herrings, based on the logic that more exotic offerings can wait until the pike 'wise up'. (It is interesting to note that Dennis Smith and Tony Lovell in their Fenland chapter adopt the reverse approach.) We apply the straightforward concept that a live fish is as totally natural a bait as possible, and we fish livebaits on new waters with complete confidence. It must be remembered, however, that livebaits do attract small pike, and a large proportion of the catch will be made up with jacks. In order to avoid false assumptions, and wrongly writing off an unpiked water, it is important to study the number, size and condition of double figure pike caught. If there are none, or they are few in number, this could indicate an imbalance in the water and a very few large fish present.

Using common rigs

There are dozens of different ways to catch pike, but here we will discuss briefly the three most commonly used, which between them produce the majority of pike caught in the British Isles today. This 'gang

of three' is the paternostered livebait, the static deadbait and the roving livebait. All three methods can be deadly in certain circumstances. However, they should not be used blindly, but under conditions that suit each of them best.

The successful pike angler will not only use livebaits, or deadbaits, or one particular method. Rather he will be a thinking man who has confidence in all rigs and baits and can change at the right times for the right reasons. The overriding question is which water responds best to which method and when. Here we can offer only generalised rules and any water may have developed its own specialised eccentricities. However, take this example of a typical Norfolk broad.

In November and December it is predominately a deadbait water. During these months it is very coloured and also contains a large head of prey fish. Fishing either a roving or paternostered livebait brings few rewards as fish are not selective at this time. By the end of December, however, frosts have caused the water to clear, and the bait fish are less active, huddled in tight shoals for protection. Now it is that livebaits begin to outfish deads. Only the man willing to adapt will catch throughout the winter.

So, in very many coloured waters where pike feed largely by smell, they are happy to feed on deadbaits. Being lazy they will probably be happier with these than livebaits. Alternatively in very clear water where sight becomes more important, livebaits frequently outfish deads.

Now, let us consider which livebait rig to use, either paternostered or free roving. Currently this is a controversial issue on the pike scene. Most experienced men prefer the paternostered, static bait to the roving one as the majority of pike caught on roving baits are small ones. However, this is almost entirely a result of the size of baits used. A large pike is unlikely to

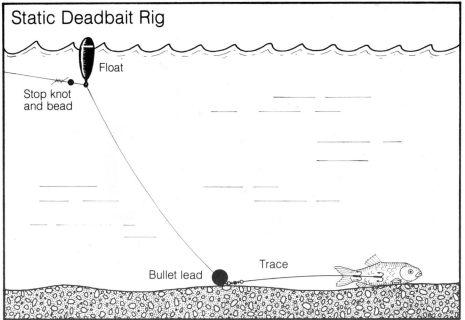

Static Deadbait Rig

Float

Stop knot
and bead

Bullet lead

Trace

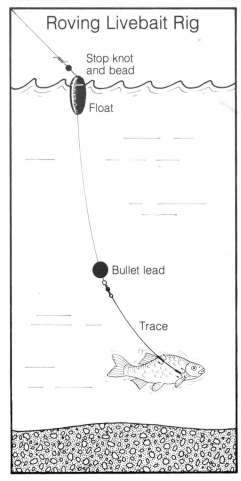

Roving Livebait Rig

Stop knot
and bead

Float

Bullet lead

Trace

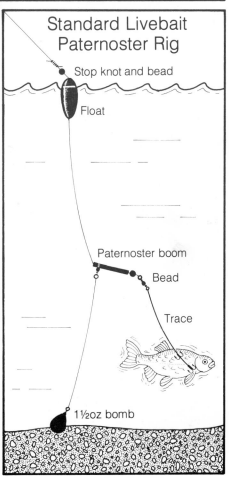

Standard Livebait
Paternoster Rig

Stop knot and bead

Float

Paternoster boom

Bead

Trace

1½oz bomb

consider a small bait to be worth chasing any distance, whereas a good-sized bait could tempt her. Alternatively if the small bait is tethered near by on a paternoster, it may represent an easy meal and might then be taken. The pike makes a simple calculation on the food reward for the expenditure of effort. There is no reason for a big pike to chase a small fish a long distance, except for occasional aggressive drives or in periods of extreme hunger.

To summarise, we would use a paternostered livebait if we were fishing an area where we knew, or were very hopeful, a large pike lived. We would also go for this rig when the weather comes in cold, and no pike is likely to waste the energy required to chase a bait. However, if we need to locate pike, especially on a new, or unpiked water, then we might well begin using a good-sized, roving livebait which will slowly search out large areas.

It should be emphasised that large baits are more effectively fished on roving rigs, as their action looks very natural. If, on the other hand, they are used on a paternostered rig, they will tow it around whatever the size of the weight incorporated. This becomes less attractive to the watching pike.

These, then are the most common rigs to catch large pike. They are all excellent at the right time and place and whilst there are many excellent alternatives, it would be an unwise man who discounts them, or who uses only one at the expense of the others.

ADVANCED DEVELOPMENTS IN METHODS AND TECHNIQUES

Vic Bellars has long been famed for his inventive approach to new rigs and methods. His approach is absolutely meticulous, even down to painting his bombs and weights camouflage green. He can be controversial, but his mind is constantly working on new techniques. Indeed in the piking world his nickname is often 'Vic the Rig'.

It has long been a tradition to use treble hooks on pike tackles, and I would hazard a guess that all other pike anglers contributing to this book do so without exception. So I am the odd man out. I do not use trebles purely because they are not as effective hooking instruments as the specially designed singles. When a pike takes my bait, I want to set the hooks, not ninety or ninety-five per cent of the time, but every time, and during some seasons I have achieved that hundred per cent hooking ratio. Furthermore, having discontinued using trebles for fifteen years, the hooking ratio to runs has never been less than ninety-eight per cent.

So, the reason I stopped using trebles was not through fad or fancy, but because I found that specialist single pike hooks were ultra efficient. If trebles had been as good I would not have needed to design an alternative. To continue in this heretical vein, I also believe that modern day pike anglers are blinded by tradition, still content to use terminal tackles that have changed little for the past 150 years.

I often ask myself why pike anglers have contributed so few innovations in terminal tackles, in comparison with those who fish for other species. All that pike anglers seem to have come up with, is merely a modification to the tackle rig that was in use at the time of the Crimean War! They have reduced the size of the hooks – some achievement!

Some say 'Jardine got it right'. Maybe. His snap tackle in smaller hook sizes is efficient, but remember it was designed for one specific method – livebaiting. Why is it so necessary to use what is virtually a Jardine rig for bottom fished deadbaits or, for that matter, any other modern method for which it was not designed? Designs can be improved however good the original. It is time pike anglers got out of the rut that they have been stuck in for years.

I admit there is very little difference in hooking efficiency between a livebait mounted on a modified snap tackle comprising two small trebles and one that is mounted on two specialised singles. But even here perhaps, the latter rig does not encumber the bait to quite the same extent, and I prefer to use singles as they are not so liable to cause damage to the pike's mouth. Unhooking, you will find, is far easier.

When it comes to bottom-fished, or buoyant deadbaits, trebles are not in the same league as singles. Normally, for mounting deadbaits, a tandem rig consisting of two trebles, or one treble and a single is the method adopted. One arm of the higher set of trebles is inserted in the bait's tail root, whilst with the second rig, a normal single hook is used for the same purpose. Both have to be buried deep in the bait to withstand the shock of casting. When a pike takes a bait, the hooks must be set by exerting a strong force on them via a tight line. The stronger the force, the better, so as to bury the hooks to the bend. With a hook inserted well into the bait's tail root, the act of striking does not exert the maximum force on the hooks alone. Rather, a proportion is absorbed, for the bait has to be moved before the hooks can take hold. When the pike has the bait clamped firmly in its jaws, more of the force required to set the hooks is dissipated, for the bait is harder to move.

Finally, as a treble has two hooks standing proud of the bait and one buried, when force is applied it is divided between three hooks rather than being exerted on one, or at the most two as in the tandem single hook rig. In a tandem treble hook rig, force exerted on these is carried to all six hook points. In order to ensure that the force exerted by striking is not partly absorbed by the bait, the hooks need to be very lightly attached, so that they pull out under slight pressure. In this situation the full force is transmitted directly to the hooks, and the less hook points the greater will be the force exerted on the remainder.

In an attempt to overcome these problems, the V.B. pike hooks now marketed by Partridge of Redditch were designed. A large single hook has a smaller single bait attachment hook brazed to its shank, on the same plane and back to back, so as to allow the larger hook to stand proud and entirely unmasked when attached to the bait. As the small bait holder is not buried in the tail root but fixed to softer flesh, it pulls out easily. Also, the small hook is as strong as the larger, just in case it too takes hold, which incidentally happens only rarely.

Unlike the usual hook placement on deadbaits, with one in the tail root and one set well back towards the tail, V.B. hooks

should be positioned to cover the bait's middle section. This helps eliminate deep hooking. This part of the bait is the area which will be enclosed by a pike's mouth when it bites. Therefore the hooks are perfectly positioned to be set without delay and usually one engages in the 'scissors'.

This hook rig has been termed 'instant strike', but this is misleading, since once a float has been submerged, or an indicator signals a take, the rod has to be picked up, followed by winding down hard to the fish and then striking. On average this takes about ten seconds and so can hardly be called an instant response. However, the sequence is more rapid than waiting for the line to run out, then waiting for a few seconds to be sure, as some are wont to do! Those using this hook rig must steel themselves to strike relatively quickly, as the hooks cover the mid-section of the bait, so any undue delay will cause deep hooking problems.

A bait with the hooks only lightly fixed into it in this way is impossible to cast. The solution to this problem is, of course, to take all the weight of the bait off the hooks when it is suspended from the rod tip, prior to casting. This problem was ingeniously solved by Alan Beat who fitted a loop at the wrist of the bait tail; another loop was fitted to the upper eye of the swivel, which joins the line to the wire trace. These two loops are connected by a strip of soluble PVA. In this way, the trace remains slack and the bait is supported by the joined loops. Later, Andy Windmill developed his clever 'flick off' device, and I designed a casting link that works on the same principle.

Tail loops are easy to construct. Any strong thread is suitable, such as the soft white Terylene whipping thread obtainable from suppliers to the boating people. No doubt Dacron line would suffice as well. About a twelve inch length of thread is doubled, and a simple overhand loop,

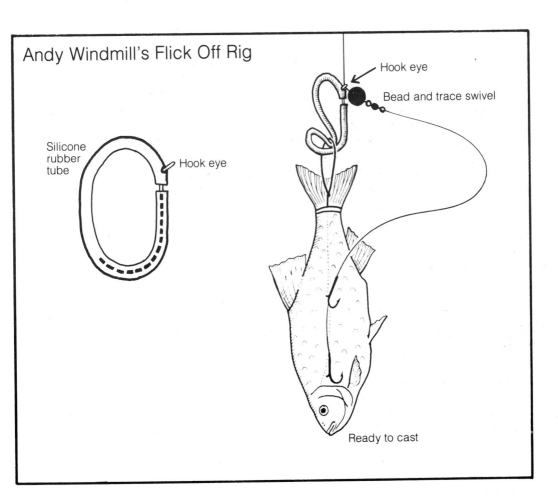

Andy Windmill's Flick Off Rig

Hook eye

Bead and trace swivel

Silicone rubber tube

Hook eye

Ready to cast

approximately one inch in length, is formed to leave two free ends. These are threaded through the wrist of the tail by a baiting needle and drawn through to seat the loop knot. Then the free ends are passed round twice and knotted. Naturally a batch of baits can be tail looped in advance of fishing and a supply kept in the freezer. I normally trim off most of the tail fin, just in case it might interfere with tail loop ejection caused by the 'flick off' device.

Neither of the two 'flick off' designs need be described in detail as the illustrations are self-explanatory. However the *modus operandi* needs to be understood. The weight of the bait is supported by the tail loop which compresses the silicon rubber circle in the Windmill design, and the double rubber in the casting link method. While the bait is in flight as it is being cast, tension exerted by the tail loop on the silicon rubber is eliminated, so it reverts to shape, ejecting the loop. This is simpler than it sounds and is one hundred per cent effective.

In the Windmill device, the trace is very slack and there is a remote possibility that it could twist and kink. For this reason the casting link method was devised. The trace is now slack but not excessively so. Ready-made casting links, with a small snap link swivel for attachment to the upper eye of the swivel joining the line to the trace, are

Vic Bellars' Deadbait Casting Link

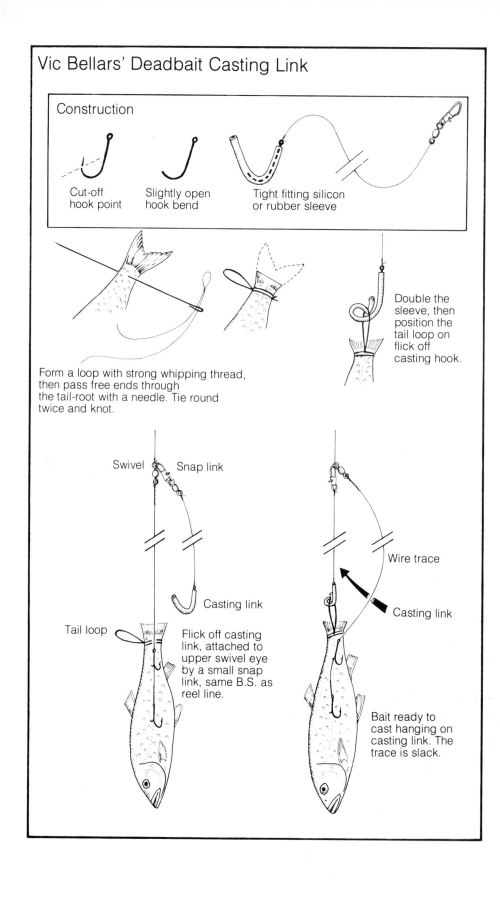

Construction

Cut-off hook point

Slightly open hook bend

Tight fitting silicon or rubber sleeve

Form a loop with strong whipping thread, then pass free ends through the tail-root with a needle. Tie round twice and knot.

Double the sleeve, then position the tail loop on flick off casting hook.

Swivel   Snap link

Casting link

Tail loop

Flick off casting link, attached to upper swivel eye by a small snap link, same B.S. as reel line.

Wire trace

Casting link

Bait ready to cast hanging on casting link. The trace is slack.

supplied by Partridge of Redditch who also supply made-up tandem V.B. hook rigs fitted to twenty pound B.S. multi-strand wire, which terminates in a strong Berkley swivel.

Of course, 'flick off' casting links like this can be made up at home. A number two or number four eyed hook has its point and barb cut off and the bend is opened out slightly. Then a length of tight fitting silicon rubber tube is eased round the bend and slid up to the hook eye. At least half an inch of tubing should project beyond the bend to allow ease of doubling. The covered hook is then joined to some five inches of line, of the same B.S. as the reel line, and a snap swivel is fitted to the other end of the link.

Small sprat sized baits are too light to compress any form of 'flick off' device. It is quite unnecessary to use tandem hook rigs – a little bait adorned with two V.B.'s or trebles is a prickly mouthful. Providing the hook is positioned in the flank below the dorsal fin, the hooking ratio to runs is excellent.

To prevent the bait flying off the hook on the cast, the trace is bound to the wrist of the tail with a soluble PVA strip or string which both dissolve quickly. The smaller bait-holding hook is inserted lightly so that it pulls clear of the bait on even a gentle strike. Alternatively the trace swivel can be passed through the bait's tail root by a baiting needle and the trace tightened until the small hook grips. With this method, every time a new bait is required the trace must be removed from the line. Some anglers will never lose a few seconds of fishing time to do this!

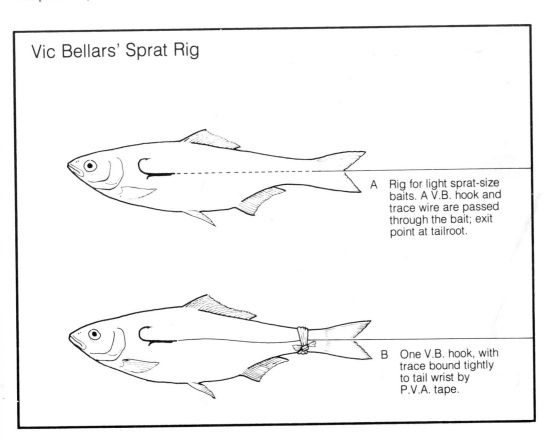

Vic Bellars' Sprat Rig

A   Rig for light sprat-size baits. A V.B. hook and trace wire are passed through the bait; exit point at tailroot.

B   One V.B. hook, with trace bound tightly to tail wrist by P.V.A. tape.

When using a tandem V.B. hook rig, you may wonder how it is possible to retrieve a bait with the hook so lightly attached. As the small bait holders are barbed there is very little difficulty, providing the bait is reeled back gently. However, Andy Goram, a Pike Anglers' Club member, solved the problem of getting the bait back every time, even after it had been taken by a pike and ejected whilst the fish was being played! All that is necessary is to pass the hooks through the bait's tail loops, before they are attached to the bait. Brilliant! Why didn't I think of that!

The hooking arrangement for float-suspended live or deadbaits, or indeed legered livebaits is the same as when using trebles. Very small baits can be lip hooked using the smaller hook on a V.B. More normal sized baits should be mounted on a tandem rig. The small bait-holding hook of the upper set is inserted in the mouth or just below the dorsal fin. This leaves the large hook clear. The small hook of the lower set is nicked in the pectoral fin root. When using big baits of six ounces or so, the larger hook of the upper set is pushed right through the dorsal muscle so that the point and barb protrude. This is most important. The smaller hook of the lower set is positioned as before.

With legered livebaits, the hooks are positioned in reverse order. The bait is lip hooked on the upper set while the small bait holder of the bottom set is nicked into the flank beneath the rear end of the dorsal fin, not in the shoulder as is often advocated. Much the same hook position can be used to wobble deadbaits. In fact, these specially designed hooks can be used for any pike fishing method and, although I imagine the die-hards would not admit it, these hooks are undoubtedly extremely efficient.

I imagined when the V.B.'s were first marketed they would be ignored. To my great surprise this has not been the case.

Perhaps they have been welcomed rather more in Europe and America. In the latter they have been used for northern pike, muskies and channel catfish. Doug Strange, managing editor of that influential magazine *The In-Fisherman* has informed me that he has had, as he puts it, 'up to sixty-three straight runs without missing a fish!'

I hope that what I have written is considered controversial. This was my intention. Firstly, I want to sow tiny seeds of doubt in the minds of those who insist on using trebles. Secondly I have written for the sake of pike themselves, for there is no doubt that single hooks do far less damage to the fish's mouth. Unhooking with V.B.'s is also far easier for the inexperienced pike man.

Finally, continuing in a controversial vein, two modern paternostered rigs have been included in this section. The normal fixed paternoster shown in books on pike angling is a tangling abomination! Even when more by chance than design the rig does not tangle, any pike taking the bait must encounter resistance from the weight of the anchoring bomb. I have been told that pike do not worry about resistance. Perhaps they do not sometimes, but on hard fished waters they certainly do!

Both the paternoster rigs illustrated allow a fish to move off with the bait in any direction without moving the bomb. What is more, the heavier the bomb the better. With the V.B. paternoster, tangling is rare, either when casting or when being fished. If the rig is reeled in quickly, the trace may wrap round the paternoster bomb link. This can be unwound by holding the hooks or bait and letting the bomb swing free. This rig is fished under tension so as to angle the sunken float away from the bomb link and the bait likewise.

The C.D. pasternoster was developed by Colin Dyson, editor of *Coarse Angler*, in an attempt to refine my V.B. rig. He suc-

Vic Bellars' Sunken Float Paternoster Rig

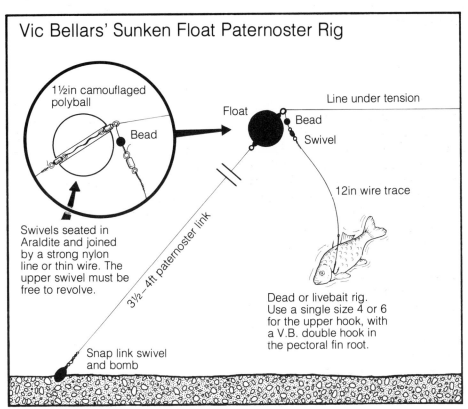

1½in camouflaged polyball

Bead

Float

Bead

Swivel

Line under tension

12in wire trace

Swivels seated in Araldite and joined by a strong nylon line or thin wire. The upper swivel must be free to revolve.

3½–4ft paternoster link

Dead or livebait rig. Use a single size 4 or 6 for the upper hook, with a V.B. double hook in the pectoral fin root.

Snap link swivel and bomb

Colin Dyson's Sunken Float Paternoster Rig

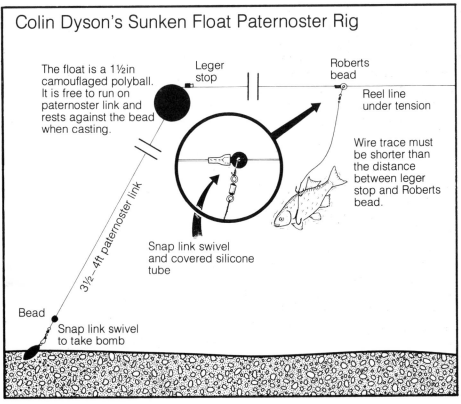

The float is a 1½in camouflaged polyball. It is free to run on paternoster link and rests against the bead when casting.

Leger stop

Roberts bead

Reel line under tension

Wire trace must be shorter than the distance between leger stop and Roberts bead.

3½–4ft paternoster link

Snap link swivel and covered silicone tube

Bead

Snap link swivel to take bomb

ceeded admirably. His rig's non-tangling character is superb. The V.B. rig was designed for bank fishing, but as Colin's rig need not be tensioned to the bomb, it can be used from a boat. Both rigs are now termed S.P.s (sunken paternosters) and can be used with both live or deadbaits, including herrings. I have purposely refrained from giving a long winded description on how to make up S.P. rigs, for I believe the illustrations are self-explanatory.

I hope the rising generation of pike anglers will abandon the old outmoded methods, and not only be prepared to experiment with the recent innovations, but also start thinking up ideas for themselves. Then British anglers will continue to be world leaders in pike angling techniques.

The Fens

The Fens, those acres of reclaimed land, laced by irrigation drains and rivers, are largely the result of seventeenth century efforts by the brilliant Dutch drainage engineers. Largely thought of as damp, bleak and misty flatlands in Cambridgeshire, Lincolnshire and Norfolk, they became famous for their pike in the 1960s and earlier part of the 1970s. There were several heroes around that time, notably Barrie Rickards, Bill Chillingsworth and Hugh Reynolds. All these men caught numbers of large pike from the Fenland drains and rivers.

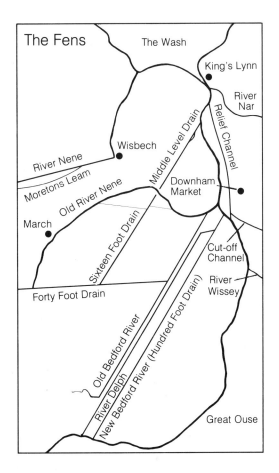

However, during the late 1970s and earlier 1980s pike fishing in the Fenlands seemed to hit an all-time low. Controversy broke out over the role of zander in the decline of the Fenland fisheries. Much blame was heaped upon this alien species, in truth there have been many contributing factors to the relative decline of the Fenlands and probably modern pollutants from farming land have played some part.

The true pike angler will not be deterred, however, for the Fenlands is a vast area, and there are many waters where large pike still live. In recent years there has been a trend towards the more northern fens of Lincolnshire, and an exploration of the Fenland pits has brought rewards for some. So, for the thinking and exploring pike angler there are still many rich pastures in the Fenlands. Indeed Dennis Smith and Tony Lovell emphasise quite strongly how superb the sport could still be for those prepared to spend some time in the area.

For our part we can only foresee an optimistic future for the Fens. As the cycle turns, one now hears of better match returns on some of the previously dead waters. The Anglian Water Authority is pressed into stocking these waters, and it

John Watson and dog taking refuge from the weather.

matters not how the food fish get there, as long as the predators have their prey. If it takes some ten to fifteen years for a water to 'return', then the 1990s may see the Relief Channel once more the centre of attention. Even now some of those waters of the 1960s and early 1970s could be producing a few large fish for the adventurous and secretive angler.

TWO INVENTIVE PIKERS

Probably the most dramatic episode in writing this book was our night flight to interview Dennis Smith and Tony Lovell. We had arranged a rendezvous at a small pub, lost in the Fens. Then, as we prepared to depart, the rain began. It poured down the whole eighty mile journey, and the wind blew the rain almost horizontally over the flatlands around us. It was waterland all right. There was water in the sky, on the roads, in the ditches, spread over the fields, overflowing the dykes, drains and rivers. It seemed that night as if the water were returning to reclaim what had belonged to it once, long ago, before the drainage engineers of the seventeenth century pumped it into defined channels.

In short, we were pleased to find the pub, Dennis and Tony, a fire, some light, good beer, and a wealth of fascinating pike lore that kept us enthralled until well past closing time. The essence of Dennis and Tony's style is to find productive waters, locate feeding fish, and present good baits to them. They have concentrated on making location a fine art, so necessary here in the Fens where there is a colossal choice of drains and pits.

They are constantly on the look-out for new waters. For example, they read the angling press, not only for reports of waters producing the occasional big pike, but also for places where good numbers of bream and roach are turning up, which in their turn will grow on good pike. Their aim is to get into a water first, to be ahead of the crowd. Only by doing things before others, do they get the cream of fishing since, under pressure, pike soon move from an area or become progressively harder to catch. They have a number of waters going at the same time. From bitter experience they have found it is not a good idea to fish the same water two days running, even if catches have been exceptional. To return on the second day is generally a disappointment and puts too much pressure on the pike.

By fishing several waters intensively, they get to know from experience when a particular pit or drain will fish to its greatest capacity under particular conditions. This may depend on cloud cover, wind direction and speed, time of the year, or even the amount of flow on a drain. Many of the drains in the Fenland area are pumped. Fishing when the water is actually being pumped is often very nearly impossible, but to fish just after the pumps start up or shut off can be excellent.

The particular weather conditions on any one day will dictate the final choice of water to be fished. For example, on a strong south-westerly wind they might choose a particular drain or, if the wind is strong, a pit. They find the pits in their area fish well in a blow, and the pit they choose will depend on wind direction. On a strong north-westerly wind one of their best pits would catch the full force, and, as this is a rare wind, they would take advantage of it irrespective of cloud or temperature.

This approach makes Tony and Dennis very sensitive to weather changes and outlooks. They will study the weather forecast leading up to each weekend and leave the final water decision until the day of fishing. Indeed, so aware are they of changing conditions that they might move

A large stillwater pike comes to the net for Tony Lovell.

once or even twice in a day to fish three waters and maximise their chances of finding feeding fish. The recurring message with all successful pike men is effort, thought and mobility. Dennis and Tony try to eliminate chance to as great a degree as possible. They demand that they get to know a water as intimately and quickly as possible, so whether they are prospecting a drain or a pit, they use an echo sounder to locate fish-holding features. Time for them is a commanding factor, and echo sounding is quick and efficient. It saves them fishing unproductive water and wasting a single hour of these weekends they so obviously live for.

Drains to an outsider can look barren, featureless rulers of water, especially in winter with savage winds ripping along them. Locating fish in such waters is vital as they may be very localised, and miles of drain may be devoid of pike. Conversely, incredible catches can be had when the pike are found. Concentrations of food supplies, spawning grounds and many other features will all attract pike to them.

Interestingly, Dennis and Tony told us that the pike are also strongly affected by dredging, and they will move down the drain in front of the dredger until at the end of the drain a large number of fish congregate. The greater the total length of dredging, the greater number of pike there will be, pushed down the drain and stacked before the dredger as it moves along. Indeed, they had some exceptional fishing on one of the major drains when six dredgers were working simultaneously.

Drains are not as featureless as they

*A Great Ouse pike boils amidst the
reed beds.*

might appear, and Dennis and Tony know
what to look for: the junction between two
drains, a ditch entering into a larger drain,
the areas around bridges, and died down
lily beds are all likely holding areas. They
stress that very subtle depth changes
should be investigated, even if it can only
be measured in inches – a pike holding
feature need be nothing dramatic. In areas
of barren, uniform water, the tiniest underwater abnormality can attract the fish.

They look for the traditional features on
gravel pits, but will often pre-bait to draw
fish to them or to a particular feature. Pre-
baiting is generally a mash of their old baits
emptied into a tub and pounded into a
rubby dubby with a branch. The slop is
ladled out, and if the wind has blown out a

strong enough undertow, the juices will be
circulated around the pit and pike will be
drawn to the area.

Dennis and Tony are immensely inventive anglers. They told us how they tackled
a particularly bad winter cold spell, when
their pits had frozen to ten inches – less
would not have been safe for this. With a
wood axe, they cut holes all over the lake,
and drilled into the ice beside them for rod
rests. They then put fish pieces into the
holes and returned the next morning. In
those holes where pre-baits had been
eaten, they fished confident of success.
They had stumbled on to patrol routes and
had only to wait for the pike to reappear,
which they generally did. As the freeze
continued, so their knowledge of the pike
movements increased, until they could
almost track them around the pit, picking
off a fish or two through each hole that

they had made.

They told marvellous tales of playing pike through the ice, fish that spin the angler around and around on the slippery surface, struggling to get a foothold. They had series of photographs of ice chips, shining in the sunshine, of pike thrashing in the tiny iceholes, and of two fishermen dressed like Eskimos. Whilst most pike men were idle, Dennis and Tony were catching pike, having fun, and building up a valuable knowledge of pike routes that would benefit them when the thaw came.

We take this opportunity, however, to advise that the most extreme caution is taken with ice fishing. In February 1985 J.B. was exploring a local lake, peering into the depths through the glass-like ice. It broke beneath him and he was fortunate to escape with no more than severe shock. In the same period M.P. saw deer walking on his favourite broad but decided to wait himself until he saw elk walk there in safety!

Equally inventive is the pair's approach to bait. Here they take pike fishing into advanced experimental fields. Their experience has taught them that even if they choose a good water and are there on the right day, the fish will still not take a bait that has caught them before and that they have become suspicious of. Tony and Dennis' argument is clear. On the majority of their pits and drains the pike have seen all the usual baits, like herrings, sprats and mackerel, and the bigger, more cautious fish will not be fooled by them. But, they have proved, even on hard-fished waters, big catches can be made by consistently keeping ahead and by providing the pike with a bait it has not seen before.

Baits can be varied in several ways. Firstly a different species of fish bait can be used. Secondly a bait can have its colour and smell changed. Thirdly a bait can be presented in a different way. The message comes across loudly: *do something different.*

Sometimes the difference needed may only be small. On many of the drains, ten or fifteen years ago the use of a herring tail would produce very good results. However, its success rate declined as fish wised up, but Dennis and Tony have caught again simply by changing to the tail of a whiting. In the same way, whereas most waters produced a lot of pike to mackerel tails, they found that a move to mackerel heads resulted in a sustained run of good fish.

Now we are moving into their range of changed baits. On most waters trout work well for one season, perhaps two, though trout is often overlooked because of its relatively high price. On little-fished waters, changed baits such as sardines and smelts often catch a lot of pike. Tony and Dennis point out that sardines are best wrapped individually in silver paper and taken to the water well frozen. They are very soft bait and once thawed become very difficult to cast any distance. Conversely, what they term as natural baits (roach, rudd and eels for example) are very tough skinned and cast well. These are highly successful, often at the start of the winter. They will often score on a pit that has been saturated with sea fish baits and even livebaits.

Red mullett have proved very successful for Dennis and Tony, and even more so have that species of sea fish called the Jack Travally. This fish became one of Dennis and Tony's favourites for several reasons. It is very tough and streamlined, and will cast through a long distance, like a bullet, even skipping a few yards across the water surface on impact to gain those few extra yards.

Kippers produced colossal bags on one particular pit, out-fishing all other baits. Kippers are normally sold in the shops split down the middle, with their backbone removed. Dennis and Tony cut the fish in half, keep the tail portion of the bait, fold the two halves together, and sew it up with

*John Watson returns a magnificent
31lb 4oz pike — the fish that fed
Martyn Page's desire to succeed on
a very difficult water.*

cotton or fine fishing line. Prepared this way, the kipper will cast thirty yards or even more. So popular were the kippers on this water, it was not unusual to catch pike on a square of kipper paternostered in mid-water, even though it did not remotely resemble a fish.

To conclude on changed baits, they suggest almost any fish is worth trying. The only species that they personally have used unsuccessfully are bloaters, smoked mackerel, shad, garfish, flyfish and gurnards. They soon came to a position where new, easily available, changed baits, of the right size and price, were becoming

increasingly rare. It was about this time that they started injecting baits with fish oils and changing their colour. They had done both of these things in the past but not regularly.

Their first experiments with coloured baits on local gravel pits were almost beyond belief. Whereas using a mackerel tail might have produced on average one run a day in a particular pit, by dying the mackerel orange or yellow or blue or red they would often get a dozen runs on the same bait type. During their first season of experimentation they used mostly red and yellow baits, but as the number of runs slowly dropped off and fish became wary, changing the colour to blue restored the catch rate.

They also found that the use of oils, either painted on a bait or injected into it, could greatly improve the chances of catch-ing pike. Cod liver oil, which is very thin even at low temperatures, was an early experiment because it is easily injected in all conditions. Herring and pilchard oil were found to be as good, if not better than cod liver oil, but would solidify at low temperatures. They overcame this problem by mixing the oil with sodium laural sul-phate and water, and injecting the solution into the bait. (The mixture is 20% oil, 80% water and 0.2% sodium laural sulphate.)

On the waters that Dennis and Tony fish, they also find the use of buoyant baits very effective, and until the pike become wary of the buoyant bait, which they eventually do, they are probably twice as effective as baits fished on the bottom. They usually make their baits buoyant by pushing forceps down to the end of the bait to make a hole, and packing polystyrene into the cavity with the forceps. Their baits are very buoyant, so it takes probably three to six swan shot to sink it all. In this way the shot go down first and the bait follows unwillingly, buoyant enough never to hit the bottom at all. The two men fear that if their bait does get to the pit bed, weed or snags could prevent it rising off and doing its job effectively. A point worth mention-ing is that baits such as sardines and smelts are usually easier to keep buoyant by using a slither of balsa-wood, as polystyrene easily destroys soft baits.

With coloured, oil-injected buoyant baits, Dennis and Tony believe that they have almost the ultimate pike bait. It is very visible to pike and can be smelt a long way off. They go fishing with a good selec-tion of baits and carry a range of bait dyes (Rayners colouring dyes) and a paintbrush with them. They paint the dyes on to suit the water they are fishing, and also the conditions of the day. Interestingly – and perhaps controversially – if Dennis and Tony start on a new water, they generally begin with their buoyant baits. To begin with a changed bait and progress to the more conventional, rather than the other way round, is a new approach to us. The thinking behind this is straightforward. The pit may already have been heavily fished in normal ways, leaving the pike suspicious. By presenting novel baits, they avoid the danger, once again, of wasting time on fruitless missions.

On the long journey home the night had dried, leaving a moon behind wispy cloud and a hint of frost on the still wet roads. We cruised steadily along the flat straight route, totally devoid of traffic. The heater was on. The dashboard lights looked like pockets of stars. J.B. remarked that he couldn't remember being so impressed with other anglers before. Dennis and Tony seemed to be men totally immersed in their sport, always thinking, always experimenting, never content. This is a common denominator with all our con-tributors. They are the most positive of pike men. Laziness, smugness and conven-tion are words foreign to all of them. Just as pleasing with Dennis and Tony tonight was their attitude to fishing – their generosity towards the feats of others, their willingness to share long built up know-ledge and, most of all, their happiness with their sport. They are not obsessive, not greedy and not jealous, they just love the sport that they are following.

ONE WAY WITH FENLAND PIKE

Keith Mottram is predominantly an angler of the Lincolnshire Drains where his successes over the years have been phenomenal. His dedication to fishing is enormous. To him a dawn to dusk session is a short one, and whenever possible he will live for days at a time on the waters. In fact he says that he only gets 'revved up' after a day's fishing! This takes some doing in winter in such bleak surroundings, but then he is a man with a purpose – to catch big pike. Such professionalism combined with both intelligence and an intuitive feel for his waters has given Keith an intimate feeling for the Fenland Drains which to many look simply dreary canalised water courses.

What Keith says reinforces in many ways the views of Dennis Smith and Tony Lovell. He agrees that the basic problem for the drain angler is to find the fish. He stresses that his tackle and methods are basic, so his huge catches must be the result of his precise knowledge of hot-spots in these apparently featureless waters. Indeed, he talks about knowing the underwater contours of many miles of water like the back of his hand.

Keith makes the point that the pike will often be packed very tightly into these hot areas, so tightly in fact that often all the runs will come to just the one rod. When the fish come on, the session can quite suddenly become electric and he will not waste one second of what might only be a twenty minute feeding spell.

We find it interesting that Keith is very much a deadbait man. True, this is often forced upon him by the regulations on his fisheries, but none the less, he is quite happy to stick to these rules, confident deads will give him the results. In fact, during three months of 1984, he landed 138 pike, all of which came to deadbaits.

What Keith has done is to give a very detailed description of three of his hot-spots in the Fenland Drains. We see each swim analysed minutely, with probable reasons given for the attraction of each to the pike. It has been suggested that hot-spots simply 'happen', that there is little apparent reason for their existence – that they are like airy phantoms. Keith rather explodes this idea. Each of his hot-spots have very real physical pike-attracting attributes. There is no mystery about them in the least.

The bend

One of my most productive hot-spots is a large bend on a particular drain in Lincolnshire. Over the years the flow has greatly eroded the bend itself, creating a wide piece of water. Looking at the diagram, I will run through the features and explain their attraction.

Upstream of the bend the water is relatively shallow at six feet, but it deepens considerably opposite the bend on the far bank. Beneath the bend the whole section of water is similarly deep, around twelve feet. There is often a good flow here that can call for a two ounce weight to hold a bait firmly on the bottom.

Now, I believe this is a hot-spot for various reasons. Firstly, during the back end month, shoals of roach and bream move into this area and stay for long

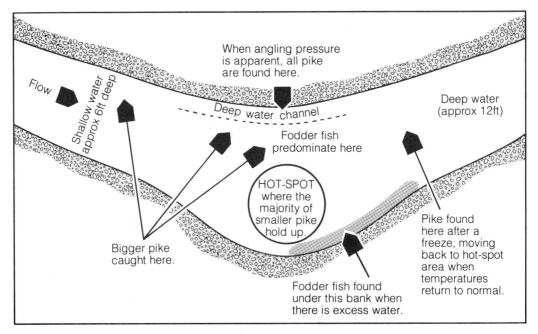

When angling pressure is apparent, all pike are found here.

Flow

Shallow water approx 6ft deep

Deep water channel

Deep water (approx 12ft)

Fodder fish predominate here

HOT-SPOT where the majority of smaller pike hold up.

Bigger pike caught here.

Pike found here after a freeze, moving back to hot-spot area when temperatures return to normal.

Fodder fish found under this bank when there is excess water.

The Bend

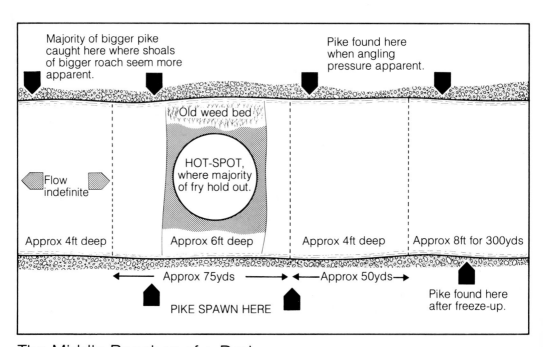

Majority of bigger pike caught here where shoals of bigger roach seem more apparent.

Pike found here when angling pressure apparent.

Old weed bed

HOT-SPOT, where majority of fry hold out.

Flow indefinite

Approx 4ft deep

Approx 6ft deep

Approx 4ft deep

Approx 8ft for 300yds

Approx 75yds

Approx 50yds

PIKE SPAWN HERE

Pike found here after freeze-up.

The Middle Reaches of a Drain

Keith Mottram holds a fine Fenland
pike. The barren uniformity of the
drain behind him indicates the vital
importance of location.

periods, acting as a magnet to the pike. It
really is an unlimited winter food larder.
Secondly, the pike like the variety of water
offered here. For example, in heavy water
conditions they can get into the relative
shelter of the slack on the near bank, out of
the full force of the dirty water. Or again,
in freeze-ups, they can drop off into the
deep water just down stream. Under
normal conditions, the bigger pike like to
lie just off the slack, at the edges of the
deeper water, where they probably have a
commanding view of the whole area.

Thirdly, I believe the bend is a hot-spot
because here the river is wide enough to
give the bigger pike sanctuary if, and when,
angling pressure builds up on them. When
the area is being hard fished, the fish move
off to the deep channel on the far bank,
which is outside the casting range of the
average angler. Fourthly, although I have

never found any evidence that the pike
stay over to spawn here, there is a heavily
used spawning ground a short way downstream in the mouth of a small shallow
side-drain. It seems likely that this hot-
spot is chosen as a convenient assembly
area or resting up place for the bigger fish
just prior to spawning.

The spawning ground
hot-spot

I call this a spawning ground hot-spot even
though pike are present all the year round
in some numbers. The area lies in the
middle reaches of the drain and from the
diagram you will see quite a depth variation over the length. Upstream the water
starts at four feet deep, shelves down to six
feet, shallows back to four feet, before
dropping to eight feet for three hundred
yards or so downstream. In fact, we are
talking more about a hot area than a spot,
as the pike use about a hundred and fifty
yards of water in all, and will be pulled

about by shoals of prey fish, angling pressure and weather conditions.

The key to the spot, the core of the place, is the large weed bed that flourishes in the summer and, despite dying back in the winter, still remains in evidence. It stretches from bank to bank and is approximately fifty yards in length. It fulfils two important functions. Firstly, it attracts vast fry shoals, particularly in the early part of the pike season, and where the fry are, the pike are sure to follow. Secondly, the weed provides the pike with their spawning beds, from which some of the pike never move far throughout the course of the year.

Another feature of the area is that the shoals of bigger roach also use it regularly.

For long periods of the year these are stationed just upstream of the weed bed, around the four to six foot shelf. Not surprisingly, this is where the majority of the bigger pike are taken from. Finally, the area offers deeper water downstream where the pike can drift to when angling pressure grows, or cold weather sets in. I do not think that angling pressure drives pike from a hot-spot, but it might disperse them around it for a while, into deeper or less accessible water.

The shelf swim

This hot-spot is easily described. It is a seventy-five yard long shelf, two and a half feet deep by the bank, gradually dipping to

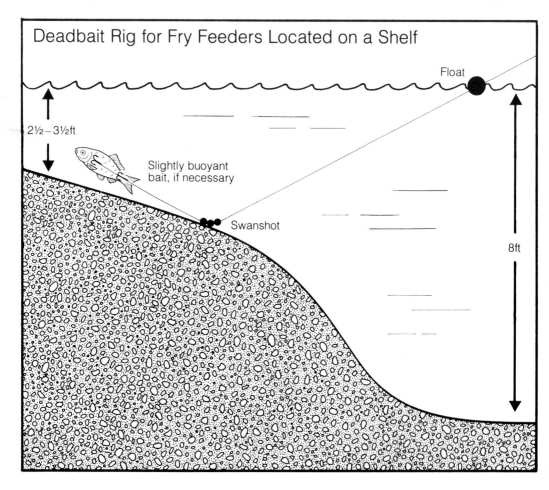

Deadbait Rig for Fry Feeders Located on a Shelf

2½ – 3½ft

Slightly buoyant bait, if necessary

Float

Swanshot

8ft

three and a half feet two yards further out, and then dropping off quickly to eight feet. Large quantities of fry are frequently attracted to the shelf and the pike follow them there to feed heavily. Also in milder conditions the big pike like to lie in the shallower water, in the silt enjoying any warmth there might be on their backs.

Let me tell you a story of a great session I had there. I had already tried the shelf on two occasions during the early season, and as the fry and, therefore, the pike had not arrived, I was unsuccessful. However, on a third visit, two anglers were just packing up and they told me the pike had been swirling up and down the shelf at intervals throughout the day. The weather was mild, the drain was unruffled and the pike had obviously been fry feeding. I was highly surprised that the men's large bottom-fished deadbaits had gone completely untouched throughout the day.

I walked the far bank along the shelf and before me big fish moved away with huge bow waves amidst spreading areas of disturbed silt. To say the least, the adrenalin started to flow. I knew I was on to some great piking. I decided to stay overnight and fish the next day, at very first light. I had a good meal, a good few pints, and settled down for a few hours sleep by the bank.

In the calm of the first light, the shoals of fry were abundant, topping in the surface film, and soon the pike began to show amongst them with large tell-tale swirls. I

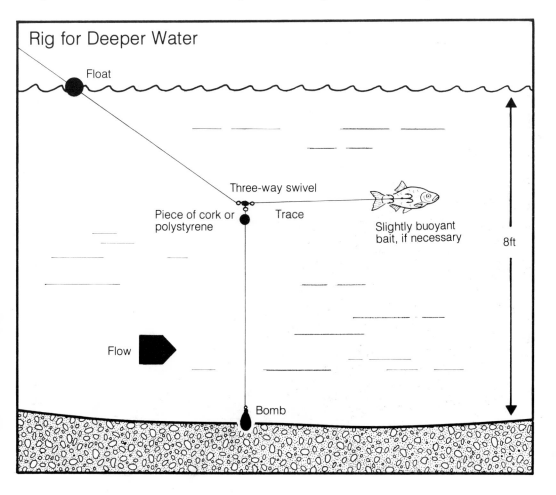

Rig for Deeper Water

Float

Three-way swivel

Piece of cork or polystyrene

Trace

Slightly buoyant bait, if necessary

8ft

Flow

Bomb

had two rods out, one fishing the shallow water over the shelf and the other positioned over the deeper water. In both cases though I had my baits near the surface zone. They were small deadbaits between one and a half and two and a half inches long, air injected for buoyancy and fished on size 10 trebles. The diagrams show the basic rig that I used throughout my time there. Results were good enough to keep me there for several days whilst I acquired fish to over twenty pounds and quite a few expensive hangovers on the way.

I found that the pike fed in frequent short bursts throughout the day, with resting spells in between. I marvelled to see these great fish come to the surface and casually take a mouthful of fry from the dense shoals, before slowly sinking back into the depths like light green crocodiles. They were so subtle, so delicate; they were more like trout gently sipping buzzers out of the surface film.

What Keith says shows the transitory nature of the Fenland Drains. Once get a dredger through the places he has discussed with us, and then the hot-spot is swept away forever.

Opposite *The head of a 23lb pike is cradled gently for a second before being returned.*

Below *John Watson brings a good Fenland fish to hand.*

Conditions

If Keith finds a fish, the only thing to concern him is when these fish might feed. He places great importance on weather conditions and air pressure. He always likes to fish before freeze-ups in cold bright clear conditions. He has even seen the pike feeding under the ice. (This ties in very much with the experience of Dennis Smith and Tony Lovell on these Fenland waters.) He stresses that drains often fish well in bright conditions, unlike most stillwaters in particular, where cloud and wind are preferable.

Towards the end of the season two or three days' sunshine lifts temperatures and trigger pike to feed, especially if they have been laid up for some while. When this happens the fish caught will frequently be covered with lice that have infested them during their long period of inactivity. At the other end of the scale, after a thaw of ice, he finds that the first or second day of fishing has frequently been uneventful. He has generally only caught fish regularly on the third day. This, he believes, is when the temperature rise has become obvious and the pike have begun to feed once more.

To conclude

Keith agrees with Dennis and Tony over changed baits. He has not done the same research into changed baits as Dennis and Tony have carried out but obviously feels there is very much a case for their use. Like them, Keith agrees that a drain fishes well when it is pumped and the current stirs the fish into activity. However, Keith disagrees with Dennis and Tony over the question of resting hot-spots. Dennis and Tony suggest it is a mistake to hammer an area and have found that to go back on the second day is to court disaster. Keith, though, will often spend days in just the one place and really exploits the full potential of any hot-spot he finds. He feels these places hold a lot of fish, and he wants to get as many as possible before they move on and once again lose themselves in the barren miles of Fenland waterways.

Lochs and Loughs

Ten, twelve, fifteen and twenty feet, and then there is an eerie apprehension, a knot tying in the pit of your stomach. You feel lost, totally insignificant. You realise the echo sounder no longer registers the bottom, that you have just drifted over a precipice, over the edge of a submerged mountain. That memory, amongst others, will always remain from a Norfolk man's first trip to Loch Lomond. Gone were the gentle depth changes of the Norfolk Broads, where a six inch variation can mark a hot-spot. Here was a rugged, dangerous and exciting environment, charged with electric atmosphere, shot through with pike that fight like gremlins.

One feels naked, vulnerable in a small boat as a storm appears from nowhere, moving down the loch between mountains which rise, claustrophobic but impressive, from the depths of the water to the limits of the sky. When the thunder echoes from rock face to rock face, and the wind rises to a roar over the endless water, it is easy to understand how so many pikers' imaginations have dwelled on the fabled tales of monsters from the deep.

We are, in part, idealists as well as realists, and both take the side of those who believe that somewhere, in some of these waters lurk huge fish. The appeal is massive. Nowhere do more natural, primitive fish exist, totally outside the bounds of man's world. For those who need a hard core of evidence, then it is only possible to say that in recent years there have been an increasing number of twenty-five pound and indeed thirty plus fish caught from Lomond, the loch at the centre of most English anglers' attention. But of course, there are hundreds of other lochs to explore in both Scotland and Ireland.

LOMOND AND THE LOCHS OF SCOTLAND

*by Gord Burton
and Frank Pennington*

From the pike angler's view, the Scottish lochs can be put into three categories – those of the lowland region, of the central region, and of the highland region. Most of the lochs in the lower border regions are shallow and the waters tend to have peat-stained coloration. Besides pike, many of the lochs hold a variety of coarse fish species. Most of them hold perch and many now hold roach, Loch Ken in particular. A number of lochs even hold tench and carp these days and the waters at Loch Maben are Scotland's premier bream water. Although many of these lochs hold trout, none of them could claim to be top quality game fish lochs. In our view it is runs of salmon and sea trout in particular that produce the numbers of big pike that are found in the more northerly Scottish lochs.

So, we move up to the lochs of the northern region, around the Highlands. These hold very little in the way of coarse fish, apart from pike and eels, but most of the waters are well stocked with trout. Pike caught from many of these Highland lochs are on the lean side, but some of the waters have produced big fish. Good examples are

A storm approaches Ardlui down Loch Lomond.

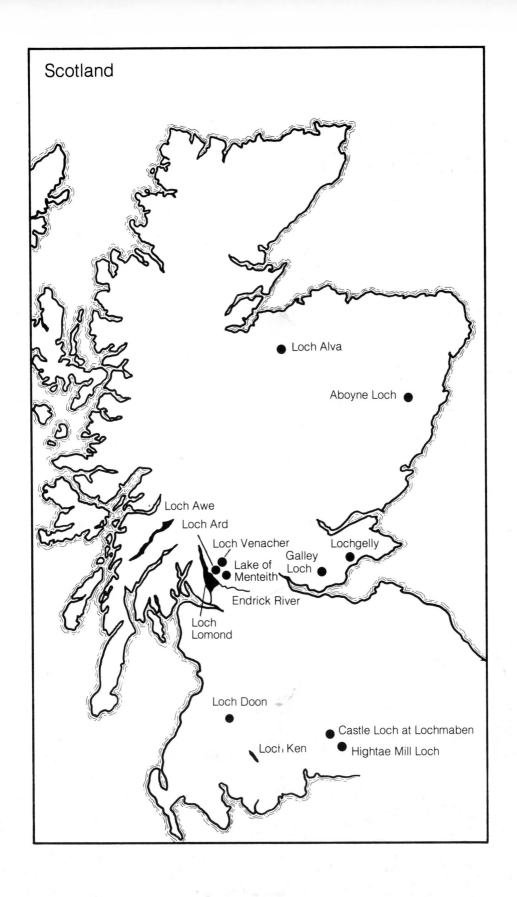

Scotland

Loch Alva

Aboyne Loch

Loch Awe
Loch Ard
Loch Venacher
Lake of
Menteith
Galley
Loch
Lochgelly
Endrick River
Loch
Lomond

Loch Doon

Loch Ken

Castle Loch at Lochmaben
Hightae Mill Loch

Gord Burton expresses the delight he takes in the Scottish lochs and their magnificent fighting pike.

Lochs Arkaigh and Oich, and both have produced pike topping twenty-five pounds.

However, it is in the central region that we do most of our fishing, on the very large lochs situated there. Lochs Awe, Lomond, Tay and Tummel are all colossal waters with equally stupendous pike potential. The first two of these waters, Lomond and Awe, are over twenty miles in length, very wide and have many bays, islands and narrows, with wildly fluctuating depths. They can appear daunting confrontations to a newcomer, but once broken down in scale, finding areas where the pike inhabit, is more simple than one would think.

Some of these central region lochs have top class game rivers connected to them with runs of sea trout and salmon that probably cannot be bettered anywhere in the British Isles. Lomond, in particular holds a variety of different species. Perch

are still quite plentiful, although they have been hit by disease in recent years. There is a massive head of roach, and shoals were once sighted that stretched for hundreds of yards. These were mostly smaller fish, but there is also a large head of fish topping the pound mark. Further, there are also large numbers of eels in the loch, and information tells us that chub and gudgeon are breeding in the Lomond waters. Sea trout and salmon run through Lomond in good numbers, and to a lesser extent there are brown trout, many of which can attain huge proportions. Most interestingly, there are huge numbers of the mysterious powan, staple diet of Lomond pike. Several years ago shoals of powan were seen finning and topping in an area off the southern shore of the loch which covered a quarter of a square mile.

Loch Awe holds huge numbers of brown trout and in recent years is regularly stocked. Back in the early 1970s there were also phenomenal shoals of perch in Awe, and any amount could be caught for bait.

The desolation of a Highland loch.

Although these fish were struck by disease and the population devastated, they are on the increase again. The rivers connecting this loch, the Orchy and Awe, are also good quality salmon waters. In our opinion, therefore, Loch Awe has the ingredients for very large pike indeed. In fact, the biggest pike Gord has ever seen on his hooks broke free on this very loch.

Loch Tay holds a colossal number of game fish due to the fact it has a premier salmon river adjoining it. The River Tay is also a top class roach water and friends have taken large bags of them, including fish over the two pound mark. For this reason we consider the Tay as a very likely venue for enormous fish.

Probably, Lomond is considered Scotland's premier pike water, and over the past few years has produced a tremendous number of very big fish. Still, other lochs are capable of turning up very big speci-mens and these lesser known lochs get very little angling pressure.

Habitat

The type of habitat preferred by the big pike of these vast sized lochs varies considerably from their smaller loch counterparts. Probably this is because they have a much wider choice both of places to live and of food supplies. These large lochs have large connecting rivers that over many years of heavy flooding have flushed silt and all manner of debris into the areas where they disgorge into the loch. This has caused large sandbanks to appear, steep sided drop offs and gouged out troughs in the loch bed. The northern end of both Lomond and Awe have large inflowing rivers and large bays adjacent to them. Many trees are brought into the lochs by floods and, for a while, float around in these eddying bays until they become waterlogged and sink, making for tackle-busting snags! The big bay in Loch Awe, by the mouth of the River Orchy is a wilderness of snags and sunken trees which can be seen deep beneath the surface of the clear water.

These vast waters have large areas of boulder-strewn loch bed, where channels run in varying directions between jagged reefs. The shoreline and the many islands have rocky outcrops that stretch out into the loch, often shelving away into deeper water close in. For the greater part of the year, the big pike will inhabit these deep underwater ledges and drop-offs, and patrol the boulder-strewn reefs. These are the perfect places for big pike to live in, where they do not have to travel far to find food.

Many newcomers fishing these huge lochs would automatically head for the reeded areas and shallow bays. On many of the lochs that we have fished these are promising-looking places, we agree, but they tend to hold only small pike for most of the year. It is unusual to catch fish above eight pounds apart from at spawning times, and only on the rarest of occasions have any good sized pike been sighted in these shallow reedy bays. So, reed beds play no part in the locating of big loch pike at any other time of the year than the spawning period, because they prefer the deep places amongst the boulders where there are no reed beds in the fifteen to thirty foot depth range. (*What Gord and Frank say here endorses research made recently in Holland and America. This stresses that in large waters the big pike move away from shallow reedy areas. Only small fish stay there, probably using the reed for protection against predators.*)

Choice of food

There has been great discussion about the food choice for big pike in the lochs, and trout are generally the most favoured by anglers themselves. However, very few anglers can obtain constant supply of good fresh trout baits, and we have seen many anglers wasting a great deal of money transporting trout to Lomond. We say 'wasting' because they have not done anything at all to improve catches.

The alternatives for the angler are coarse fish, smelts and varying sea fish species like mackerel and herring. We have taken big loch pike on a wide variety of different baits, for example, roach, rudd, perch, chub, gudgeon, dace, carp, trout, mackerel, herring and smelts. It does seem then, that the pike in these lochs do have a very catholic taste.

One important point found in the diet of Loch Lomond pike is their undoubted preference for powan. Gord has on many occasions examined the stomach contents of pike from the Loch. (These fish are spawning casualties or pike killed by the salmon anglers.) Twice perch were found, once roach fry, on one occasion an eel, at another time a mouthful of sticklebacks, and one pike contained five trout. Every other pike Gord has examined contained powan, often several fish.

We have found that Lomond pike tend to be the most fussy of loch fish, and on many of the more outlying lochs the pike will take almost any bait offered to them. The only time Lomond pike fall readily to most baits is during the spawning season.

Gord has worked out a very comprehensive bait pattern for the Scottish lochs and his findings have certainly been proved by conclusive results. Over a period of regular fishing throughout the seasons of the year, it is very noticeable that silver-scaled species of bait far outfish dull sombre-shaded baits like carp or perch. On Lomond, we feel this is due to the predominance of powan in the pike's diet. So

Opposite John Watson unhooks a big fish taken from an Irish lough. Notice his use of multipliers and the padding on the boat floor to prevent damage to pike.

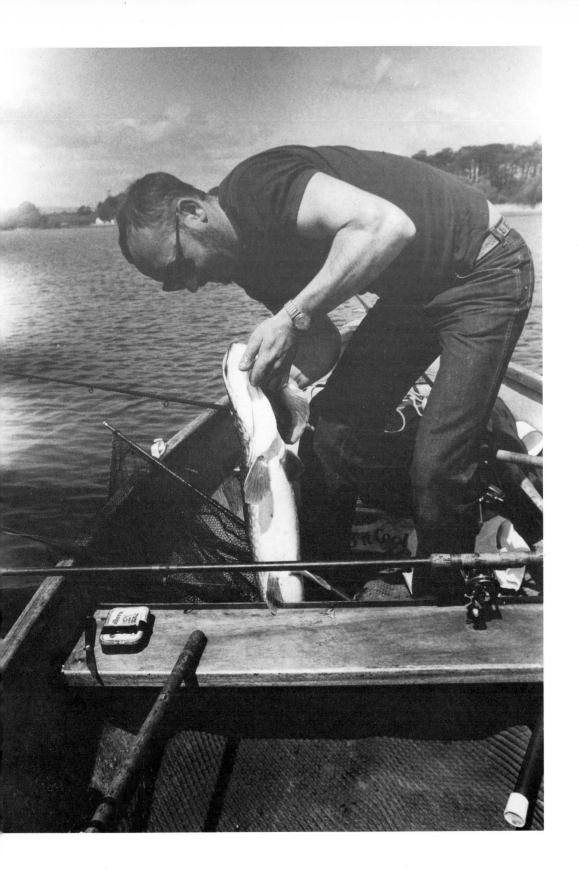

silver-scaled fish like roach and dace do produce a majority of pike. However, and this is important, more dully-coloured baits like carp and perch very often produce the largest pike. Frank in particular has taken a number of twenty pound plus pike on carp baits, and carp have certainly accounted for at least one thirty pound plus fish.

The pike year

We will start with the post-spawning period. Once the big pike have performed their annual spawning rituals in the shallow bays, they will feed with a vengeance to build up condition. During this period they will fall for a wide variety of both live and deadbaits as they begin vacating these areas on their way to the preferred habitats in the deeper more barren areas of the loch.

As the summer approaches, their feeding times take on a marked pattern that is often only broken by certain light and wind conditions. Their choice of food becomes far less varied in the warmer months and we have found that deadbaits produce far less pike than at any other time of the year. This does not mean to say we do not use the method – invariably we have one rod out with a deadbait on it. In fact, Gord's big fish of twenty-seven pounds was on a deadbait which does seem to sort out the very largest fish.

Throughout the summer period anglers must be anchored up over their selected area in time for daybreak, as the dawn period can be dynamite when the big pike go on the prowl for food. Many times we have not had a chance to get a second rod into action before a run has developed.

Nights are spent afloat on the lochs during the summer. Frank has a boat with a fully fitted out cabin and this is a major change since our early days of big loch fishing. During the summer it is often light

enough to start fishing at 4 a.m., so being afloat throughout the night is a massive advantage. These mad daybreak feeding spells can go on for a few hours and a big haul of pike will often be taken. By mid-morning the pike generally go quiet, but in dull conditions with a fresh wind blowing they will be caught periodically throughout the day. The wind no doubt has a cooling effect on the water which keeps them active in what are usually bright calm conditions. As a rule blazing hot days and flat calm waters are not productive in terms of catching big fish, however Frank once accounted for a big catch including twenty pounders by fishing a free swimming live carp only two feet down over deep water.

During the summer these big lochs are buzzing with fish activity. There are large numbers of sea trout and salmon running through the lochs on their way to spawn, and the roach and perch are easily located near the surface. On Loch Lomond the powan are frequently sighted finning in the distance. Many times as dawn has broken we have seen the surface of the loch dimpling with fish. Powan in Lomond often stay down deep during the midday period, but they will rise up in the water as darkness approaches when they will feed in the surface layers, often very close in to the shoreline. Big pike have been caught in small shallow bays on the edge of very deep water, and there is no doubt that they have been attracted into them by the movements of the powan.

As well as the dawn period, the evening right into darkness is also very successful for big loch pike. This merely re-enforces the importance of staying by the rods from dusk right through to mid-morning. Unfortunately many anglers we have observed fail to do this and their results suffer because of it. Starting out several hours after dawn and packing up a few hours before dark is not the way to be a successful

Frank Pennington holds onto a thrashing loch pike, showing that a multiplier is the tool of the boat angler.

loch pike angler.

The high summer, especially if the weather is hot and dry, can bring about algae blooms, when the water will become thick with minute green particles. This in turn clings to boulders and reed beds in thick clumps. When a breeze blows, the thick algae is blown off the reed beds and boulders and then fishing becomes a problem. These green clumps of algae will clog up along the line and get stuck on the baits. When reeling in, the line can seize up and jam in the rings, preventing the angler retrieving any further. The miserable stuff has to be stripped off the line before fishing can begin again. Gord first experienced this algae problem when fishing on Loch Awe in 1974. Many of the country's leading pike anglers fail to get amongst big pike, probably because of the problems of the algae blooms.

In some recent seasons, we have experienced algae blooms on Loch Lomond, and it also affects to an even greater extent the low border region lochs. From our extensive fishing experience, we have found that big loch pike do not like this algae, and very few fish are taken while the bloom lasts. All the advice we can give is to try and find an area free of the bloom, sometimes where a river pushes into the loch and the water is more cool and more clear.

When the summer is coming to its close, the winds start to blow over the lochs and temperatures can drop suddenly. Then you will find the algae will disappear very rapidly. This is the time when we have had some tremendous catches of big pike. It is as though the big pike have lain doggo during the algae blooms and then gone on the rampage as soon as the water has cleared again. We were once on Lomond just after the bloom had died down and Frank took a bag of pike to over twenty-two pounds whilst I hammered out a large catch of pike to over twenty-four pounds further down the loch. We took well over forty pike in two short sessions. We hope you see now the vital importance of being on the loch at the right times.

During the autumn big loch pike are caught in numbers and will fall readily to both live and deadbaits. They congregate in the vicinity of the river and stream entrances where the game fish run to spawn. The pike feed so avidly that they are often caught throughout the day and all tactics can produce big fish. It is as though the large amount of food fish in these locations send the pike wild. Indeed we have seen the surface of the loch alive with running fish. Gord once went a few yards up an entrance stream where he could see masses of sea trout and salmon in a tiny pool only ten feet in diameter and four feet deep. It can easily be seen why so many big pike frequent these places.

During late autumn, Scotland's notoriously bad weather starts to rear its head and lashing gales and heavy rains are often experienced. Wild weather conditions often bring about wild feeding spells and so we stay afloat in all but the roughest conditions. We know from hard experience just what our boats are capable of, and both are good seaworthy crafts!

The heavy rains flood the rivers, which in turn means coloured water pouring into the lochs. As we said earlier, big loch pike will not tolerate dirty or coloured water and will move away from this. For example, when the River Endrick floods into Lomond, thousands of acres of the southern region can become the colour of tea, as so much silt is pushed into it. To give an example, when once fishing out from a river mouth we were hammering out big fish, but as the area began to flood with coloured water the pike stopped feeding. When the boat was moved and re-anchored back in clear water, big fish continued to be caught again.

After the heavy autumn rains and floods, the loch will settle down again and become clear in the vicinity of entering rivers and streams. As winter approaches, activity on these big lochs will start to dwindle and they appear lifeless as very little shows on the surface. Game fish have made their runs into the rivers to spawn, and perch and roach cannot be found. However desolate this may seem, big pike can still be caught by those anglers prepared to fish on through atrocious conditions. What makes the fishing bearable is that we both feel that winter is probably the best time for an enormous fish. Loch Lomond has produced a number of fish over thirty pounds, to an enormous thirty-five and a half pounds during recent winters.

Even while we rate these winter months, the weather conditions can get so wild as to prevent regular fishing. Also, the feeding habits change dramatically. No longer are the pike those ravenous bait-chomping fish of the late summer and autumn, now they are very finicky towards their prey. We experience very few of the scorching runs often known in the warmer seasons of the year.

Dropped takes now become a regular occurrence. Often live and deadbaits are retrieved and found to have been tooth-marked or even badly chewed, when we have had no indication of a take whatsoever. Pike have obviously swum up to these baits, chomped into them hard and then let go without our ever guessing their presence. Even scaling down on hooking rigs and bait size – to size ten trebles and four to six inch baits – have not helped at

Lomond pike fight dramatically well. Perhaps the clear water is a reason, or that they are a slim fish built to pursue fast-moving prey.

all. Sometimes the slightest indication of a take has been struck at and on occasions this has paid off. We wonder if these pike caught during the late autumn had been feeding hard before lying up during the harsh winter months when they feed little indeed, lying semi-dormant in the deeper water.

Although fishing is very slow, there have been occasions when pike have been caught in some numbers, in extreme conditions. Some pike were caught from Ken when most of the water was frozen over, and even the fish were very cold to the hands! On another occasion Gord took a number of pike by deep-trolling plugs on lead-cored lines when all the surrounding landscape was covered in thick white frost. Frank caught a massive pike on livebait fished against an area where the loch was frozen over, when the float fish bait was taken under the ice itself.

Now, during the winter months, Frank will ring the weather centre for a forecast before setting off on a northern journey. Before, during the early explorations, we went North no matter what the conditions, because we wanted to find out how these waters fished during the winter. Sometimes we arrived at a loch only to find large areas totally frozen over and we had to break our way through with the boat to reach a clear place to fish in.

Preparations

When travelling hundreds of miles every few weeks, careful preparation is of utmost importance. The whole success of a trip depends on the ground work that has gone in beforehand. Good quality live and dead-baits are essential for both of us, and Frank in particular is very fussy indeed about our bait selection. We ensure that all our baits are in first-class condition before we start

our fishing.

Much has been discussed regarding tackle for big loch pike fishing and we are both unanimously in favour of stepped up gear. Not only are big loch pike powerful fighting fish, but their habitats on these vast sized waters are far more rugged than one meets under general English conditions. Occasionally you will be able to fish with standard gear in certain surroundings but, taking the season as a whole, heavy tackle is essential.

To be at all successful on big lochs boat fishing is the only possible way of doing things, and an echo sounder is also, we feel, an absolute necessity. Time is tight and an echo sounder cuts all manner of corners.

Tactics

Firstly, we always use one livebait, paternostered upwind from the boat. In most cases this will be over the deepest of our selected points, over anything between twenty and thirty-five feet of water. Fish have come from depths well in excess of thirty feet on Lomond, Awe and Ken, and big pike spend much of their life in these depth ranges.

A deadbait set up will fish out over another point and, if we place it in a static position, it will be on the shallowest ledge around us. Many times, however, it will be presented on a heavily greased line, so that the bait can drag along the bottom in a wide arc, continually searching through the area.

A third rod will also fish a livebait in one of two methods, according to conditions. It will either be paternostered in a shallower position than the deep set rod or it will fish on a heavily greased line as a free roving bait. When free swimming a bait, especially

Opposite A furious pike boils amidst spray and weed, desperate to shake the hooks free.

a lively chub, we will steer it to work along ledges throughout the whole swim, searching out the pike as it goes. Baits can be sent long distances in this way and cover large areas.

For the greater part of the year, we prefer good sized deadbaits and anything up to one and a half pounds are regularly used. The livebaits vary slightly, but usually one rod will fish a smaller sized bait, let us say four to six inches, and the second will have on a larger bait. This might be anything in the region of ten ounces, but in the winter this bait will also be scaled down to something much smaller.

Both of us these days have our own boats and we generally fish alone. In this way, we can fish three rods with natural baits, and then bring into action a fourth rod for plug fishing. The whole area around the boat will be systematically worked through, using a variety of plugs. If two anglers were in a boat together with three rods each, fishing would be somewhat cramped.

Fishing these varying approaches, the whole area is worked, and if any feeding pike are on the prowl, we feel there is a great chance that they will be caught. We will concentrate on one area for anything up to six hours, from the dawn start through to the morning. If no big fish have shown, a complete change in tactics is demanded. We might, for example, change to trolling. A long stretch of loch will be chosen and worked through using both nylon and lead-cored lines. Usually, when trolling during the heat of the day, the lures are worked deep, often below thirty feet. The chosen route will be worked over for two hours in the hope of finding an area where pike may just be feeding. We have yet to catch a very large pike on the troll, but we do know it has proved a very effective method for others.

A favourite tactic is to drift over a hot-looking area and work it through using a wide variety of plugs and spoons. This is a

neglected method, but when catching plenty of big pike we appreciate it greatly! Natural fish-patterned plugs are the most effective fish catches in the clear water of these lochs. Gord has taken three twenty pound pikes on plugs with a perch-like finish to them. Another method we have used to catch good pike is trolling float fished live and deadbaits. This tactic is used over a similar route as we chose for trolling with the artificials. A big pike was taken on the first trial of this method on Lomond.

An effective boat drill is vital for the times when these big loch pike are mad on the feed. The rear stabilising anchor must be lifted when a big fish is hooked. While it is being played the other rods must also be controlled. All equipment must be ready at hand – camera, hooking gear and scales. Immediately a big pike is boated get it

unhooked, weighed, photographed and returned as quickly as possible, because very often other big fish will be about. We have boated six large pike in just one hour's fishing, and three of these were twenty pound plus specimens. If we had not been properly prepared, this sort of catch could not have been made. Most anglers that we see catch a large fish then pull up the anchors and head to the nearest shore for a photography session. Thus, they miss any other large pike that are probably still feeding in the area that they have located.

We stress that these mobile versatile

methods are generally for summer and autumn. During the winter a more static approach is adopted. Little moving around is done. The days are very short, so we often sit it out a whole session on one hot-spot. Newcomers to these big waters must never underestimate the fickle environ-ment that they are fishing in. They must be prepared in every way. Treat the lochs with respect when out afloat and always carry a lifejacket. Remember it is a working angler who gets the results from these great waters, and the fighting pike of Scotland make all our efforts very much worthwhile.

Opposite *Gord Burton displays a long lean Lomond fish. Around him lie the tools of the troller's trade.*

AN APPROACH TO IRISH LOUGHS

by George Higgins

The man who trolls knows solitude. He goes afloat in the knowledge that out there somewhere in the vastness of an Irish lough lie great pike. He hopes that his search by trolling will reveal one to match the monsters of legend, but he enjoys the hunt passionately, and until the big one turns up he is content with lesser pike.

'There's bigger in it than came out of it,' said the man at the bar, almost dipping his nose into the shamrock etched on the head of his Guinness. We knew what he meant. 'Sure, wasn't the beast glaring over his

shoulder, and wasn't his tail still dragging the road?' He repeated an often told story, and yes, he could just manage another pint.

When he was a young man, the now old Charlie saw a great pike enter the shallows at spawning time. 'I could see the wake of him from the top of the hill,' he recalled. 'Liam was clearing his land down by the

Larry Nixon holds a deep-running Irish fish of 23lb, hooked on a trolled copper spoon.

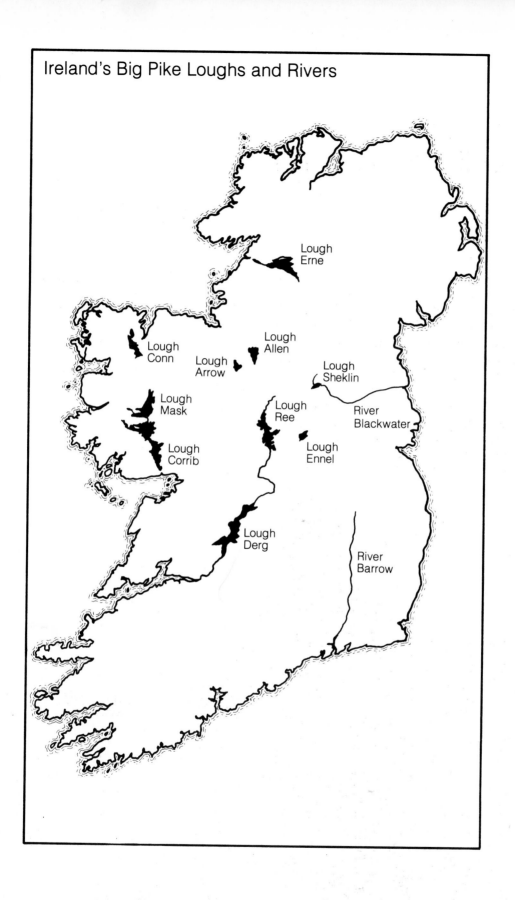

Ireland's Big Pike Loughs and Rivers

Lough Erne

Lough Conn

Lough Allen

Lough Arrow

Lough Sheklin

Lough Mask

Lough Ree

River Blackwater

Lough Corrib

Lough Ennel

Lough Derg

River Barrow

A hooked pike displays its anger.

water's edge, and when he caught sight of it, went for his gun and shot the pike stone dead. It was the biggest pike you could ever imagine, the length of a cart and a half,' he paused for effect. 'It was,' he continued, 'and it weighed eighty pounds. Never seen the like of it before nor since.'

He finished his tale and, taking the charred pipe from his grizzled lips, spat with conviction into the brambles. But I wanted to hear more. 'What did Liam do with the pike?' I asked. 'Do with it?' old Charlie repeated. 'Why, he cut it up into chunks and salted it down. It lasted him and the family all the year.' I believed him, even allowing for an extra pinch of salt! I believed him because I wanted to. Stories like this fire the imagination and I thrive on pike lore. Maybe that is why I fish the big loughs, and why I choose to troll them

in search of big pike, where they hunt and feed, rather than sit and wait for them to find me.

Our boat inched its way from beyond the edge of the shelf, where the water plunged to fifty feet and more, on to a tack which skirted the tail of a rocky island outcrop. Three lines sized the ruffled surface in the wake of the boat. The restless action of two copper spoons and a herring transmitted the message that they were working well to the nodding rod tips. We were relaxed. The day was a pleasant one and we talked about earlier successes. My long narrow copper spoon, one of Alex Dickey's creations, was on trial, and wavered its way close to the boulder strewn shore.

The sudden rasp of my reel startled us. An exceptionally fine pike exploded from the surface and hurled its great bulk high into the air. The hazy August sun glinted on its broad mottled flanks, and a shower of crystal spray cascaded in all directions.

A defeated fish sees the sunshine of day.

I recall all this in slow motion, as the pike froze for a moment in mid-flight, before crashing back into the lough. It launched itself skyward twice more, but by the time Roy had his camera ready for an action shot, the pike had gone down deep. We had drifted off the edge of the shelf and there was no stopping it as it tore line off the reel in a succession of powerful runs and dives. Only many minutes later did it come grudgingly to the net.

There are several ways in which the search for big pike can be approached, when fishing the vast expanses of Irish loughs. As there is no closed season, you can ignore the vast open spaces if you want to during the spring time, and choose a sheltered shallow bay where the pike come in to spawn. Here you may fish with conventional methods from the shore and be successful. Alternatively, you accept the challenge, take to a boat, and experience the angling thrill of a lifetime. Every nook and cranny of our waters are there to be explored by the man willing to troll. I cannot pretend it is easy fishing, but then anything truly appreciated takes effort. From May onwards, the majority of pike have gone back into the open body of the loughs, and it is the trolling man who will take them.

When trolling with two or three men to a boat, success should be measured by the boat catch. It is rare for everyone to do well on the same day. If personal blanks are unacceptable, then fish on your own from the bank, for trolling is a team effort. Remember that it would be presumptious and wrong of anyone if he accredited every pike he caught on the troll to his own skill. The skipper, be he on the engine or oars, puts the boat over the pike for a start. Who reeled in the other lines to avoid a tangle? Who threw out the anchor when it was most needed, and who netted the pike once it was beaten? In our team, *I* may blank, but *we* seldom do!

Boats and engines are the tools of the trollers' trade. They are something to blame it all on when things don't work out. I can both love and hate them all in the same day, but I trust them with my life.

The traditional Irish lough boat design was not arrived at by accident, and a sturdy seventeen foot wooden clinker-built craft remains the best tool for the job. However, because they are expensive to buy and costly to keep up, many anglers settle for a glass fibre equivalent. We once had three boats, two wooden and one glass fibre. One of the wooden boats was stolen and sunk by poachers who saw us as a threat to their operations, the other was written off in a storm but later repaired with glass fibre, and the third, a twin skinned bath-like simulated clinker boat in G.R.P., gets the most use and the least maintenance. We prefer to spend what little time we have actually fishing.

A reliable engine is essential. We have a Seagull and a Yamaha, and there are other very good ones on the market today. A clutch, recoil starter and reverse are useful assets. The Seagull lacks all three features of the Yamaha, but it starts when required and runs day long trouble free. Three and a half horsepower is adequate, unless you are in a real hurry. Trolling speeds range from slow to slower still. If the wind allows, take to the oars – it's peaceful too.

So, the boat has an engine, oars, and should carry an anchor with sixty feet of rope tied to a bow ring, a baler, and a waterproof cover for all the gear that is inevitably carried. Boat rod rests are invaluable, especially for the skipper. I have seen none to match the one I have made. It is infinitely variable between forty-five degrees and the lough surface. A simple rod rest can be constructed from a length of strong cord tied between the two seats. A

loop holds the butt of the rod which is cantilevered out over the gunwale and restrained by the rowlocks. This method, of course, can only be used under power.

The weather on the loughs can be unpredictable and especially as winter approaches, first priority is good warm loose clothing, protected by an efficient wetsuit. The best combination I have come across is a generous pair of oil rig quality over-trousers with elasticated waist and ankles, over a pair of Derri boots and a PVC smock, with welded on hood, no studs, no zips, just a drawcord for the face opening. A two piece suit is more versatile than a one piece.

Where the boat plies its trade is a secret of success in trolling. Pike location is a problem for anyone new to a lough, but there are rules which, if followed, will put the visitor in line for a big pike. Deviation from the rules and experimentation can follow as knowledge and proficiency are acquired.

Big pike are lovers of rocks and boulders. The water trolled will be in the ten to twenty foot range, and distance from shore may range from a few yards to several hundred. An echo sounder will be invaluable, otherwise it could take years to become familiar with the depths over which you fish. The sounder does not guarantee success but it does take a lot of the guesswork out of it.

I have not fished long enough at depths of thirty feet or more to draw any conclusions, but I admit to having little confidence in trolling very deep water. Shelving contours occur more frequently in water up to twenty-five feet than they do further down, and most Irish loughs tend to bottom out in the forty to sixty foot range. Every lough has been in the process of silting up since its formation, and the bottom of the deeper water is covered in feet of mud. Pike are creatures of boulders, reeds, weeds and snags, that provide cover from which to launch an attack. A smooth

George Higgins nets a big fish for Bob
Templeton. The bait was a trolled
perch.

mud bottom is devoid of this cover, and I
can't for a moment imagine why pike
should be in frequent residence there. The
temperatures at depths over thirty feet, for
most of the year, if not all of it, will be very
cold, and I would expect any pike inhabiting such depths to feed even less than the
pike of shallower waters, and goodness
knows that is infrequent enough.

Big pike holding areas are shelves and
drop-offs, and it does not automatically
follow that, say, the fifteen foot mark is the
ideal depth. It is if the depth drops off
sharply, but likewise it could be a plateau
where the depth all over is fifteen foot. To
fish over such an area is to wander aim-
lessly.

Any headland or point is a sound choice,
but trolling takes a boat past pike quickly
here, and it is a good idea to give them at
least three passes before moving on. Still,
do not flog a spot to death. If no strikes are
forthcoming, move. It is feeding and
hunting pike we are seeking. Overkill of an
area does not bring dormant pike on the
feed, and part of the allure of trolling is the
ever changing scene. Each bay and headland presents its own problems, and

nothing is still in trolling, not for a moment.

Islands will draw the troller off shore, and are well worth attention. If a pinnacle of rocks can be detected rising up from deep water, then these sunken islands can be trolled around in similar fashion. Find them and pike will not be far away.

When we consider other factors which have an influence on successful trolling, water clarity comes high on the list. Acid or bog fed loughs, in a settled state, are the colour of whisky, Bushmills to be exact. Colour, by the way, is the only thing they have in common! Big bog loughs do not suffer from algae blooms to the same degree as the richer alkali waters surrounded by farmland, where nitrates from the soil are washed into the lough. Rivers in flood stain a bog lough, but the staining is localised, and can and should be avoided.

I have deliberately not mentioned baits

Andy Barker leans into a 24lb Irish pike.

and tackle until now, for I consider that once a venue and the time of year are selected, a good boat and engine are booked or bought, and you have an idea of where to start your search for a big Irish pike, then you are ninety-five per cent of the way there. The last five per cent is entirely your own responsibility.

Rods are well down the priority list. Use whatever you prefer. Long rods can be a nuisance in a boat, and I find a nine footer is manageable. Reels are more important. I prefer a Hardy Silex centre pin for trolling bait. It's totally reliable, and there are no adjustments to seize it up at the crucial moment. I have got used to the right-hand wind, and playing a big pike using finger control on the rim is a real joy. The bait is not cast, but lowered into the water, and the forward motion of the boat takes line off the reel. This ensures that the bait trolls tangle-free. For spoons and plugs, I use a Cardinal 55 fixed spool reel. On occasion we may stop and cover a bay by spinning,

Roy Smyth shows a magnificent 25lb Irish fish, taken on a trolled herring. The vast Irish waterscape shows behind Roy.

and we always have two rods made up in the boat. With practice, two can control four rods. When there are three or four of us in a boat, we use one rod each.

Whatever your tackle, total reliability is the first essential, followed by whatever takes your fancy. It would be sheer madness to come all the way to Ireland for the pike of a lifetime and lose it because your ten pound line snapped. No trolling line should be less than fifteen pounds B.S. You may see fit to thank that piece of advice, when a twenty pound projectile explodes from the surface with your lure clamped in its massive jaws. A strike on the troll can alarm anyone who is not expecting it.

I could, with conviction, say snap a plain copper spoon on one rod, and a three or four ounce fish on the other rod and you need never look back. But, that would be an oversimplification. Of the twenty-nine pike over twenty-five pounds that our group called the Pikers have caught, twenty were taken on the troll. Ten fell for bait, nine for spoons, and one to a plug. Roy Smyth's biggest pike, weighing thirty-one and a half pounds came to home-made copper spoon. Other lures like the Toby Salmo have scored some notable successes. I know too, that some of the patterns of copper spoons made by Alex Dickey and myself are accounting for some nice pike in English waters, and I can see their use becoming more widespread.

My favourite home-made copper spoons are polished or burnished plain copper, and allowed to tarnish to a warm pinkish hue. What could be more pleasing than to hook a big pike on a spoon of your own making? Tinsnips, a small round headed hammer, a drill, a junior hacksaw, an old block of wood, some emery cloth and a flattened piece of domestic copper pipe are the basic requirements. The craftsmanship comes with practice and a good eye for design. Like all collectors of pretty things, I have acquired hundreds of spoons and plugs of every conceivable type over the years, and many have been trolled for miles in their time.

Moving now on to baits, herrings are the most successful for trolling, followed by perch and roach, but bream, trout and several other species have all caught big pike. Mackerel do not troll well. The success of the herring, I believe, relies on its tendency to fall to pieces on the strike, for here lies the biggest problem when trolling bait. Unless the hooks can be moved when

those majestic jaws clamp on the bait, then the pike is likely to release the lot once it has realised that all is not right with its latest victim. It is the big pike that have struck hard, feel like a heavy log, and allow themselves to be winched towards the boat, that are the problem. We have had some great pike on beneath our rod tips, and then, sickeningly, they just let go. Having clamped on to the bait, I believe that their sheer bulk makes any strike on the part of the angler useless.

The main culprit is the top hook on the trace, be it a single or a treble. It carries the weight of the bait, and the normal method is to pierce both lips, which often makes it necessary to decapitate the bait before the hooks move at all. Repeated striking to move the hooks from the bait into the pike is not the answer, but there is a solution. A five amp fuse wire looped through both lips of the bait gives us something else to hook on to that will break on the strike. The

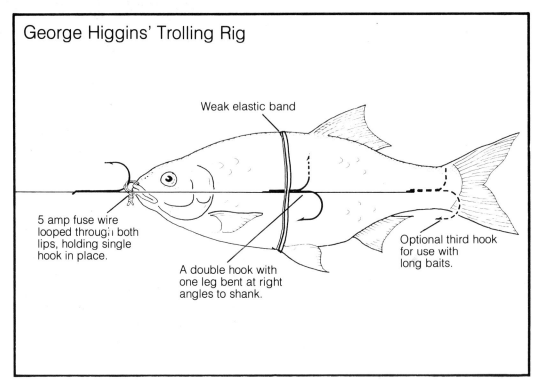

George Higgins' Trolling Rig

Weak elastic band

5 amp fuse wire looped through both lips, holding single hook in place.

A double hook with one leg bent at right angles to shank.

Optional third hook for use with long baits.

George Higgins holds a sleek Irish twenty pounder which fell for a trolled Toby.

number of turns, threaded through using a darning needle, depends on the amount of drag generated by the bait. A couple of twists stop the hook from falling out.

In addition, a double hook with one leg bent at right angles to the shank is pushed into the side of the bait, and held there with a weak elastic band. Two hooks in a series can be used like this, depending on the length of the bait. No bend is put in the bait for the delicate hook hold would not maintain it, and it is not necessary, for the bait will revolve without further assistance. This method is a fragile set-up. Hit the bottom and the bait is gone. Hit a pike and the wire breaks, the side hook pulls out of the bait and, if we are lucky, into the pike. For anyone considering multi-hook rigs, don't. It only takes one good hook hold to boat a pike, and I just can't bear thinking of the consequences of a pike, hooked on a multi-hook rig, by some chance breaking the line or trace.

A Sharps ball-bearing swivel on the trace is a must, and this is assisted by a half moon piece of roofing lead folded over the line above it, to act as both an anti-kink and a weight. The bait will fish six to eight feet deep, and that is generally deep enough. Twenty to thirty yards between bait and rod tip is sufficient. Pike often ignore noisy engines to take the bait fished on the shortest line. Very often the first bait over the pike gets the strike.

When I recall all the big pike we have caught trolling, which could never be reached from the shore, I am convinced that trolling is the best method for locating and catching the big pike of the larger Irish loughs. I am certain trolling gives the greatest thrill that any angler afloat can ever hope to experience. Try it. I know you will agree with me, and will want to go where the wild pike roam free and fearless, to track them down in the places that they themselves hunt.

TROLLING ENGLISH STYLE

Dennis Smith and Tony Lovell are far from being Fenland anglers only and have had great experience of trolling throughout large English stillwaters. They make the very valid point that English and Irish waters do vary considerably in important ways. Irish loughs tend to be warmer, shallower and often clearer than their English counterparts. As a result, Irish pike can see a lure from greater distances, are not likely to be down so deep, and are often more active fish, willing to chase food for longer distances.

Still, to them, trolling is the only method to explore the very large stillwaters of this country. They stress that it is hard to find pits large enough for the technique, as they need trolls of several hundred yards to be efficient. Trolling, therefore, is very much an approach to reservoirs in particular, and on these inland seas it is a better bet than merely casting from the boat around a thirty yard range. Then, a pike follows a bait, but soon sees the boat, is alerted and wheels away before his mind is made up. A three-quarter mile troll, on the other hand, will give him all the time he needs.

An echo sounder is essential to give them a clear picture of the bottom contours they are moving over. They use soft actioned ten foot rods on trolling rests fitted with Ambassador 9000 reels and eighty yards of lead core line. Their lures, whether plugs or spoons, are almost invariably big and they aim to work them along well-defined features at a speed best suited to the lure's action. There is nothing hit or miss about the method for Dennis and Tony. It is as exact a science as they can make it. They strive to know the speed of the boat, the depth the pike are lying and/or feeding at, and the pace the lure works best at. Into this combination, they then need to integrate such variables as wind speed and direction and the force of underwater currents. They are constantly thinking, re-assessing and experimenting until they hit pike.

As important as boat control is boat stealth. Rowing is preferred to even an electric motor and, as they say, 'they go soft on the oars', even wrapping the rowlocks in cloth to deaden any noise or vibrations.

They prefer to use spoons to plugs – big spoons built to the Higgins Irish style. They will be home-made so that they can afford to risk them a pike's tooth away from snags. As to coloration, they like

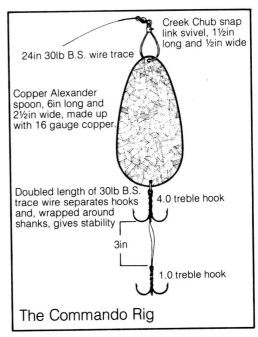

24in 30lb B.S. wire trace

Creek Chub snap link svivel, 1½in long and ½in wide

Copper Alexander spoon, 6in long and 2½in wide, made up with 16 gauge copper.

Doubled length of 30lb B.S. trace wire separates hooks and, wrapped around shanks, gives stability

4.0 treble hook

3in

1.0 treble hook

The Commando Rig

bright chrome, copper or gold, and it must be bright and in no way tarnished. They take a can of Brasso on board with them to polish the spoons freshly spick and span as they need them. Not even preparation the night before is meticulous enough for the two men. They passed on two last tips: when the pike show signs of coming short to the spoons, the pair use what they call commando hooks attached to the lure (see diagram above).

And finally, when they locate pike activity or a particularly interesting feature, they mark the place with a plastic bottle tied to a rope and anchored. These golden areas can be nearly impossible to find again in deep windswept waters without some homing device being planted or a compass fix being taken.

1 *When it all came right. Steve Harper and Martyn Page display pike of 22lb 4oz and 28lb 15oz.*

2 *The mood of the Fenlands. A bivvied*
  angler sits it out.

3 A yellow herring and natural herring
  compared.

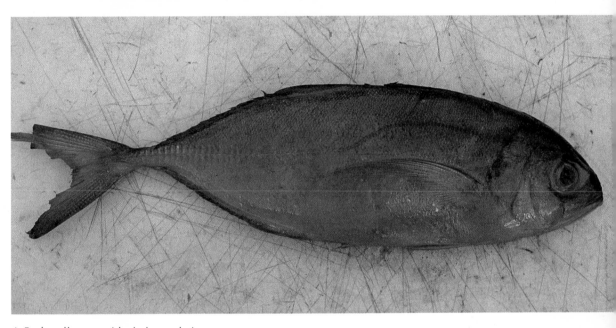

4 Red mullet — an ideal change bait.

5 A yellow mackerel and natural
  mackerel compared.

6 Herrings dye the most vivid red.

7 Another fine change bait — yellow tuna.

8 A coloured herring proves successful.

9 Above *Stuart Martin cradles a fabulous pike, weighing 36lb 1oz.*

10 Below *Gord Burton heaves into a tail-walking double.*

11 Opposite (top) *John Watson smiles wryly at a tooth-marked, rejected bait as he sits it out on Lomond.*

12 Opposite (bottom) *The bait goes back into the bay once more.*

13 Right *Perhaps the most beautiful Scottish water is Loch Awe, seen here straggling between the hills and mountains of Argyllshire.*

14 Below *Frank Pennington holds his 25lb 12oz Lomond fish, taken during a summer evening on live carp.*

15 The majesty of Lomond is captured
in the snows, heather-clad hills and
chasing clouds.

River Pike

There is something about our larger, faster rivers which seems to frighten the average pike angler. Perhaps he is content to sit with his herring, fishing at sixty yards in his local lake or gravel pit, catching the only big pike present, a fish which has been caught by all his friends and himself at least twice! This is a little harsh maybe, but river pike fishing requires an entirely different approach. It is not a lazy man's sport, and is often for the loner. Because our big rivers can be challenging, they are certainly the most neglected pike fishing you can find.

Mile upon mile of British river has never seen a pike angler's bait, and we can understand the awe-inspiring problems of locating and capturing pike in waters that can be twenty feet deep, with several feet rise and fall of tide, which are constantly coloured, fast flowing, many yards across, and are several miles long. However, in this modern day of competitive pike angling, surely here is pike fishing which has thrived on neglect and is just waiting to be attacked?

Some of England's waters are justly famous for their pike fishing. A premier example is the Hampshire Avon, with its thirty-seven and a half pounder from the past and thirty-five pounder this year. The rivers Severn, Wye, Stour, Shannon and Waveney are all capable of thirty pound monsters. We expect the Trent and the Thames could produce similar fish, and there are countless rivers with even richer

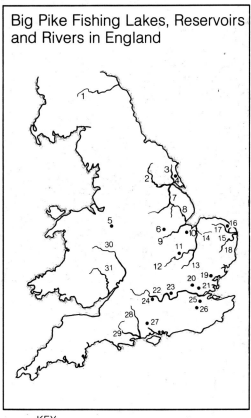

Big Pike Fishing Lakes, Reservoirs and Rivers in England

KEY

1	River Tweed	17	River Thurne
2	Yorkshire Ouse	18	River Waveney
3	River Hull	19	Abberton Reservoir
4	Hornsea Mere	20	Tring Reservoirs
5	Cheshire Meres	21	Lee Valley Pits
6	Rutland Reservoir	22	River Thames
7	River Trent	23	Colne Valley Pits
8	River Witham	24	Oxfordshire and
9	River Welland		Berkshire Pits
10	The Fens	25	Medway Valley Pits
11	Grafham Water	26	Bewl Bridge Reservoir
12	Great Ouse	27	Broadlands Lake
13	River Cam	28	Hampshire Avon
14	River Wissey	29	Dorset Stour
15	River Bure	30	River Severn
16	Norfolk Broads	31	River Wye

Rivers are often clear enough for big fish to be located visually.

pickings, where salmon, trout and large pike thrive together, such as the Test or the Tweed.

There are then so many rivers, with so much potential. And yet we have heard anglers so often say that they consider pike grow larger in stillwater. These anglers say that the energy required to maintain a position in fast flowing water could otherwise be expended in growing. Yet this does not seem to be the case, for is not one of the most famous waters in the country, the Thurne, tidal and often subject to strong flows? No – rivers have a history of big pike which denies such a stillwater bias. These large rivers are quite capable of thirty pound pike and even greater ones.

There is a shadow, no, a dark cloud, hanging over all our rivers. It is mankind's poisoned gift to his environment. Water is abstracted for use on the land, and the banks are straightened in order that the river flows more quickly to the sea. By these two actions, our upper rivers are slowly lost as they become narrower, shallower and less capable of supporting the fish we require. The straighter banks also encourage a faster, more uniform flow, perfect for spreading the effects of a pollution to a greater length of the water. It may take some fifteen years for a pike to grow to the size you desire but only one fifteen second spillage to kill it and every other pike in the river. For these reasons we cannot understand why every angler does not support the country's only organisation which protects our waters, the Anglers' Co-operative Association (A.C.A.).

BIG RIVER PIKING

by Mick Brown

Over the last couple of seasons I have noticed a definite upsurge in interest in river piking. Even so, it would still be true to say that the majority of rivers in this country are only lightly pike fished. After talking to many successful and experienced pikers I find that many of them rarely, if ever, fish for river pike, often not realising the vast and largely untapped potential of such waters.

To cover the variety of rivers I have fished over the last fifteen years or so would require a whole book rather than one chapter. Their variety in terms of size and flow is considerable and their differing characteristics are quite unique. The tiniest river I have piked is the Little Arrow River in Herefordshire – barely six feet wide and less than a foot in depth. Taking six pounders from this sub-tributary of the River Wye holds as much fascination for me as pulling 'doubles' from a bigger river.

At the other end of the scale comes the mighty tidal Severn and the lower Great Ouse, whose dimensions are such that a man might take a couple of minutes to row a small boat across them. In between these extremes the variety is endless and amongst my favourites I include the turbulent Hampshire Avon in the South, the Somerset Axe, a small flow-controlled river in the South West and the gently flowing River Bure in the East. Some have given me success, whilst others I have yet to beat. All have given me pleasure.

My intention is to restrict this chapter to the larger rivers with medium to heavy flow and in particular I shall be referring to the Severn and Wye. These types I like to refer to as 'real' rivers as opposed to the sluggish rivers of the East which often lack the flow which brings life to the water and, in my opinion, interest to the fishing. It is this flow that makes river pike and the methods of fishing for them just a little different from general stillwater piking.

To illustrate the nature of these pike I would like to refer to an observation made some years ago as I walked the banks of the River Wye on a freezing cold January morning. Passing a gin-clear shallow section in search of some deeper water to fish my deadbait, I disturbed a pike of about seven pounds from under the bank. It moved across into the current and casually took up a position in the streamy boulder-strewn icy cold rapids. There it lay, completely unperturbed by the heavy flow. In relating this and other similar sightings to fellow pikers, many express surprise that pike should be in such water. What they fail to appreciate is that pike were living in these conditions thousands of years before the reservoirs, drains, estate lakes, gravel pits and broads were made by man, and before flow control slowed down other rivers. The fast water pike are the real thing in their original environment.

Coping with relatively harsh conditions of flow and flood, these pike are probably a little hardier and generally fight a little more obstinately than their stillwater brethren, although I can't help feeling that this is a point quite often exaggerated by

Mick Brown holds one of the most beautiful pike we have ever seen. It weighed 24lb 12oz.

some writers. Most pike caught anywhere before temperatures plummet in the late autumn fight well anyway, and if any difference should be noted it is that river pike still fight reasonably well even in midwinter when stillwater pike sometimes acquire that 'wet sack' reputation.

A couple of memorable instances spring to mind to illustrate this point. One in particular is of a beautifully marked seventeen pound Severn fish tail walking and taking line in the centre of the heavy flowing river on a grim February afternoon. I would have been happy with that fight from a July caught fish. Then there was the eighteen and three quarter pound Wye fish that would not give up. This fish struggled to the very lip of the net after I had taken it on a livebait trotted through a

churning salmon pool. When finally in the net, the fish gave a final thrust that pushed me back in surprise. The fish leapt skywards, did a perfect somersault and landed, luckily, back in the net with a mighty splash. What a fight from a back end fish which, incidentally, missed the magic weight by spewing up a big roach, a herring and a trout in the process. I should hope I've learnt enough over the years not to let such a minor point bother me unduly. Magic memories will make my old age more bearable.

So here we have it, hard fighting pike in relatively tough conditions which, compared to their stillwater counterparts, cope with ever changing conditions of flow, drought and flood. The pike of these rivers have no easy passage and neither do the anglers who seriously fish for them. There are a few quiet backwaters and easy banks here and there but the general nature of these rivers consists of steep, uneven

A big river pike makes its final surge for freedom.

banks, often littered with trees, bushes and dense undergrowth. If you like to set up a bed chair and brolly and sit behind three rods on optonics, I should forget river piking here and now. The key to this fishing is mobility. This ideally suits my restless nature which compels me to keep moving even on stillwaters. Anglers will often approach similar situations quite differently and the approach, methods and tackle I will now describe for catching river pike have been developed to suit my own desires on the rivers that I fish, and of course may not suit everyone and every river.

Location is a key word that will crop up in every chapter of this and any other angling book, and to my mind this is usually the main aspect of any piking that requires consideration. Once located, most pike are fairly easy to catch, although river pike can be an exception due to the awkward places they can get into. The location of fish is greatly assisted by observation. This will include observing pike themselves and also their effect on other fish. In addition we can benefit by observing features and situations which may attract pike.

Actually observing pike in big rivers can be difficult but sightings will occasionally be made and more so in the clear shallow reaches. My most memorable sighting came unexpectedly on the Wye when I was eel fishing during one close season. Two huge identical pike, each well in excess of twenty pounds, slowly glided side by side underneath my rod tip in two feet of clear water – sisters perhaps? My great plan to catch them came to nothing when the foolish actions of a certain angler caused us to lose the water. Even so, I try to gain some knowledge from everything I observe. The type of water that they were moving into quite surprised me due to its shallowness and strength of flow, and I am sure that such information gathered over the

years make that little difference on the day when the experienced angler catches and the relative novice doesn't, even if they use identical tackle and bait.

If fish cannot be seen then feaures which attract pike often can, and again more so in the clearer shallower reaches. Many features cannot be seen but can be found by various means such as plumbing or trotting a float with a one ounce bomb suspended beneath it. Every advantage should be taken to observe features when a river is running low and clear for, even if it is of no benefit on the day, this information will be useful on a future visit.

What features should you look for? The traditional approach of finding quiet slacks and lay-bys, side streams and gentle glides is a good start but this really is only the beginning of the search. I have read in old angling books that ninety per cent of river pike will be found within a few feet of the banks and in the common belief that this is correct, anglers who have little or no experience of river pike will be positioned with this in mind; however, just as many will be located further out, taking advantage of sunken trees and branches, boulders and streamer weed and natural faults in strata – very common in the River Wye. Not all features hold pike but if prey fish are nearby then there is a good chance they will.

So, the first thing you should be aware of is where pike are likely to be, but whether one can effectively fish these places, particularly from the bank, is another matter. The use of a boat opens up all sorts of opportunities but access is not always easy on this type of river. I try not to worry too much about these out of reach features for I have, over the years, developed the opinion that the pike are not always resident in them but often use them as stopping off points as they move around the river in search of prey. For example, on the Hampshire Avon I have noted from a

Mick Brown prepares to lower a herring into an underbank swim. Notice the distance he keeps from the water's edge.

bridge, pike making their way across the river by moving from one bank of streamer weed to the next. On several occasions on this river, pike have picked up my baits from the near bank and taken them straight across the river to under the far bank in one fast run. I am sure that this movement between features is not restricted to river pike but it makes one realise that a pike could arrive in your swim at any time, and could account for the many occasions when I have taken a fish just as I was thinking of moving off after a long fishless wait. Was it there all the time or had it just arrived?

Having found a couple of features, let me give typical examples of how they may be exploited and in each case show how observations made on a fishless day can pay dividends on a future visit. The first instance came many years ago on the Hampshire Avon. Whilst on a chubbing holiday during September I noticed an incredible feature in a generally shallow fast run of water. The gravel bottom simply fell away into a deep hole immediately downstream of a dense bank of streamer weed. I could clearly make out a patch of clean gravel where something lay regularly – a barbel perhaps or maybe a big trout or, as I hoped, a big pike.

The following January I was back on a piking trip and the river was pushing through hard. I was troubled to find anywhere at all to drop a bait when I suddenly remembered that feature. With colour in the water I could not see it but a quick poke with the rod tip and I soon found the spot where the streamer, which was still quite dense, ended. A very large herring was dropped into the hole and it held well even though the surface boiled and churned. Half an hour later I was away and battling with a fat sixteen and three quarter pound pike which put up a fight I'll never forget. There is a nice sequel to that story too, when I went down the following January for three days. The only run I had was in that same swim, slightly downstream, and I caught the same fish – this time at twenty pounds eight ounces – my first twenty. I have caught many pike from such observations but of course not all were big fish.

On another occasion I got lucky again by finding a useful feature. While I was trotting a bait down the stream I happened to notice the wavering streamer weed, right next to me, part and reveal a sheer ledge which was for most of the time hidden under the weed. An ideal place for a big fish to lie, I thought. With gin-clear water I had spooked anything that might have been there on that occasion so I planned to fish it properly on another visit.

The next weekend I crawled into the swim on my hands and knees and lowered a big scad deadbait very gently over the ledge as the weed opened up. I set the rod up for audio and visual indication and went into the next couple of swims to trot a livebait on my second rod. An hour later I watched the bobbin drop back an inch or two and as I picked up the rod the line zipped upstream as a pike made off with its meal. Five or six minutes later, after a tricky netting operation on a narrow muddy bank, I was admiring a magnificent twenty-two pounder lying in the crunchy frosty grass of the December morning.

So far I have only talked about lies holding one or two fish but as with all waters, rivers have their hot-spots. The most memorable river hot-spot I ever encountered was in the tidal Severn. A huge sunken tree in twelve to thirteen feet of water was stretched nearly a quarter of the way across the river and yet not a twig showed above the surface. The head of big

pike that lived there was unbelievable. The number of double figure pike taken from that swim was phenomenal and I personally took dozens up to twenty pounds three ounces. I am sure there are many other treasure chests simply waiting to be discovered.

Other hot-spots occur on these big rivers during the winter floods when backwaters and side streams fill up. The numbers of pike that shelter in them from the fast, dirty water can be quite staggering. These swims are usually packed with masses of fry as well as hordes of sizeable prey fish which makes for ideal piking. Sport can be hectic and I have taken up to nine double figure fish in a day by exploiting such situations. I have also taken many pike to nineteen pounds from these areas of pike concentrations in the pitch black. I think that we can only begin to understand what goes on beneath the cover of water and darkness.

As a final point on location I would say by all means observe and search out these places for yourself but never forget that non-pike anglers have a lot of useful information too as they often see a lot more pike activity than the pike angler, as their methods obviously attract pike to their swims. Whenever I walk along a new stretch of river I will stop and talk to as many anglers as possible about the way their fishing is affected by pike, and one soon builds up a picture by hearing of fish taken from the hook and keep nets being attacked. Keep nets full of fish act like magnets for pike and I have taken several fish by dropping a livebait alongside another angler's net.

Having located pike or potential holding places, the river piker is now faced with tackling up for them. The choice of method is often dictated by a knowledge of the pikes' feeding preferences. Some rivers are predominantly livebait waters whilst on others both live and deadbaits score well. I must admit that this is a point I have yet to

*Neil Glover cradles his first 20lb pike
which fought right to the net.*

fully understand. Bait availability is the
next factor which will affect possible
methods to try. On a typical day I like to be
armed with a variety of baits to give me
more options, for river piking is all about
versatility. I like to go out with livebaits of
varying sizes and a selection of sea and
freshwater deadbaits, not forgetting some
plugs.

With river piking my approach is to
make a slow progression along the river,
exploiting every possibility as I come to it.
The first thing to note is the colour of the
water. If the water is gin-clear and you are
clumsy enough to spook a big shoal of chub
from the swim, chances are the big pike
waiting for one of them to step out of line
will move off with them. I approach a pike
swim no differently than I would approach

a small river chub swim.

For river pike the clearer the water the
better as far as I am concerned and my
results bear this out. Pike may be seen quite
regularly feeding in a coloured river but
they rarely seem to find my baits under
such conditions. Coloured water generally
coincides with flood water and, on most
stretches that I fish, snagging up can be
almost unbearable at these times. Imagine
you have got up three hours before daybreak, driven seventy miles and walked a
further mile, then arrive only to find that
the river has started to rise and colour
overnight. In the first hour you snag up
and lose your best three livebaits which
you have spent hours fishing for. That is
the sort of frustration one has to put up
with to be a river piker.

More often than not though the river is
in a fishable state and each swim will vary
from one day to another according to river

level. Some swims are made better by extra water and some become unfishable. As one approaches each swim it is wise to take a few minutes to decide where to cast a bait and which bait and method to use. For example, the first swim may be a deep glide with the option of trotting baits well out into the river. It could take a dozen trots or more down to get to know the varying depths and position of snags and streamer weeds.

I would get to know the swim by trotting with a biggish deadbait lip hooked so that I could sink and draw it back. In the time it takes me to get to know the swim I might take a fish or I might not. I might then rest the swim for five minutes and drop my deadbait in the edge, perhaps near to a tree stump or behind a boulder while I have a cup of coffee. Again a fish may come at this stage.

Now it is time to play my trump card. Having worked out depths, lead required and positions of snags, I will put on a decent livebait and send it through on the best course. It is much better to use a deadbait to sort out the swim than waste a livebait which would not stand the continual casting required. The livebait will very often score where the trotted deadbait did not, but only when presented correctly. If I don't take a fish on that occasion I may return to the swim later that day armed with valuable information about it. Once learnt I never forget these details which means that on future visits I can fish effectively from the word go.

The next swim I come to may have a huge fallen tree, half in and half out of the water – a dead certainty to hold pike, but not so easy to fish. A paternostered livebait is always a good prospect in this situation. The obvious problem is the extent of the sunken branches. Using a standard paternoster rig, but with the hook trace removed, I will make several casts near to the surface branches, making a slow retrieve, feeling for the underwater branches. The lead link has three granny knots in it to enable me to pull for a break if necessary, only to lose the half ounce bomb in the process. This is actually my standard practice on all lead links for all types of fishing.

After a few casts I will have a reasonable idea of where to drop a bait without snagging these branches and some idea of how much pressure I must put on any pike hooked there to keep it from being lost on them. In this situation I would choose a smallish livebait that enables a quick strike and is less likely to snag. The more violent movements of a big bait increase chances of snagging, and the slightly longer delay in striking could mean the pike has gone well into the tree branches with the inevitable possibility of a breakage.

In this situation I may well decide to fish a large deadbait on the bottom if I have an accurate picture of the snags, indeed on the Wye and the upper Severn when the river is running clear the snags are visible to the angler anyway. I always float fish my deadbaits when river piking as the float gives an accurate indication of bait position and tells one if the current has shifted it, possibly into a snag. Because of the snagging problem I rarely leave a deadbait for more than an hour. As I have said before, this knowledge of the swim is invaluable for future trips.

The next swim may be completely different yet again on a river like the Wye or the upper Severn. We may now be confronted with a large slack with deep water well across the river. If I had sufficient livebaits I would prefer to livebait the swim, but with so much water to cover, and some of these swims are huge, I would exhaust my supply before I had fished it out. Here I would probably decide to sink and draw a large deadbait. Sinking and drawing deadbait is a very underestimated method and, when used, is often carried out with little thought by many anglers.

A fallen tree provides an ideal pike holding area on the River Wye.

Some of these large slacks can be riddled with debris on the bottom, including weed, branches and boulders. Continual snagging and bringing in baits festooned with bits of rubbish is a good way of putting pike off so I make a slight modification to my rig, if necessary. The idea is quite simple but very effective – I use a float. I simply set my float so that the bait is at rest about eighteen inches off bottom. Apart from not snagging up I have the advantage of a very, very slow retrieve and the opportunity to stop my bait altogether. The baits act much better if the swim bladder is left intact and sufficient swan shot are added to just sink the bait.

When I get to know a swim well I will often, summer or winter, run a plug through it – although at £4 to £5 a time for the big plugs I prefer to be very cautious and probably not as effective as I could be if money was no object. I have been a be-liever in plugs for river pike ever since one day, years ago, on the Hampshire Avon when a 'thing' followed my little three and a half inch jointed lure right to the bank before I ran out of line. I don't believe I have seen a bigger pike to this very day. Even so, I have taken river pike to nineteen pounds ten ounces on lures with many river doubles, and I reckon in proportion to time put in with them they are certainly not a last resort method, especially during the warmer months.

No chapter on river piking would be complete without reference to boat fishing. The wealth of fishing opened up by being afloat is colossal. Ideally, a boat is suited to the quieter deeper reaches but really the only limitation is how much of a risk you are prepared to take. Fast rivers are danger-ous places to boat fish and I don't think I need say more on the obvious matter of safety. Fishing on the big weirs is opened right up with a boat and these are a lot less difficult to boat fish than is first apparent.

Boat fishing for river pike could

command a chapter in itself but I will only mention here my favourite reason for getting afloat. This is to trot livebaits further out in the river than I could possibly do from the bank. The beauty is that I simply drop the bait over the side, trot down, retrieve and repeat. Without a take, one livebait could last nearly all day as no casting damage is done. When a take does occur the thrill of bringing a fish back against the flow from as much as eighty yards is tremendous. When it's an upper double there is little in fishing to compare with it for me. Boat fishing brings new dimensions to the fight. Not only do they move away from you, but they go under-

neath and behind you! The boat also helps with those snaggy swims which can now be approached from different angles.

Up until now I have mentioned little about bait size and pike size. I would like to be able to say that there is an optimum bait size for catching numbers of pike and similarly big pike, but this is not so. I am sure there is no such thing, for the pike's moods and preferences are ever changing with seasons and conditions and sometimes angling pressure. I simply fish to catch as many pike as possible, but in doing so try to recognise what is producing the better fish during a given period. One week it may be a static seabait, whilst a few weeks later only a big livebait will make a big fish move.

I am not sure that size of bait is the only criterion anyway. When pike have a preference for livebait I would rather have a

The Tweed, one of the most beautiful of British rivers, is home for some very large pike. Unfortunately, many excellent areas are reserved for salmon and trout angling.

lively little four inch dace, darting all over the swim, than a three quarter pound bream with no life in it. I have taken many good pike on big baits but many more on small baits, including a memorable twenty-one pound eight ounce summer fish from the Severn on a three inch roach, the last bait in the bucket, when my big baits had taken a dozen fish to fifteen pounds. Fortunately, this preference for a given size and type of bait only occasionally applies and most times river pike, being the opportunists they are, will go for anything presented carefully to them, especially if dropped right on their noses.

This brings me to an interesting point. Sometimes I come to a situation where I know pike are almost certainly in the swim from previous experiences, yet I can't get a take. What I do is hit them hard on the head with my livebait by weighing it down well and trotting through the swim four or five feet over depth. By taking a different line each trot I must inevitably bounce a bait off a pike's head eventually, thus inducing a response. I have had so many fish like this that I am convinced of its effect. On the other hand, I have snagged up so many times in doing so that it's not all plain sailing. I have also used this over depth livebait method for trolling on the slower rivers with great success, taking pike to twenty four pounds twelve ounces.

River piking when carried out in a serious manner is then a very physical and strenuous aspect of angling and undoubtedly a young man's sport. It really is a different world from lying in a bivvy, waiting for an optonic to sound on a pit or reservoir. Of course, there is a lot more to stillwater piking than this simplification but I am saving all that for my old age when my legs cannot stand the stress of climbing up and down the banks of the Wye or Severn all day long. Before that day comes I have only one wish — for a fast river 'thirty'. They are a rarity indeed but turn up once in a while. The awesome tales told by the old salmon anglers have convinced me that here and there in rivers like the Wye and Severn are superb fat salmon-fed pike that will match anything the trout reservoirs have to offer and it is this dream that makes me put up with the pains that go with the pleasure of river piking.

PIKING ON
THE WESSEX RIVERS

by Bob Mousley

My pike fishing career started back in the sixties. At that time my activities centred around pits, reservoirs and, in later years, the fen drains of Cambridgeshire and Norfolk, so apart from lochs I have sampled a fair variety of pike habitats. I mention this because if anyone were to ask me now what type of water I find most enjoyable to fish, my answer without hesitation would be rivers. I do not mean slow flowing ones like the Thames or my native Great Ouse, but those of the Wessex area, famous for producing specimen fish of various species from their faster moving waters.

All the South Western rivers have produced upper thirties at some time in their history, the most notable being the previous English record of thirty-seven and a half pounds from the Hampshire Avon. Unfortunately this was a long time ago – 1944 in the case of the Avon fish – and sadly a lot has changed since then. The rivers have declined and the worst affected is the Avon itself. However, it is still possible, although extremely rare, for them to produce fish over the thirty pound mark. The need for stricter conservation on these rivers is long overdue.

The prejudice displayed by most salmon anglers and bailiffs is to me something straight out of the Dark Ages. I have just been informed of a marvellous fish of thirty-five pounds from the Royalty Fishery, caught by a pike angler but killed by the bailiff because he did not want 'a fish like that in *his* river'. Unfortunately it will take a great deal to change such attitudes. In fact I do not believe it is possible.

Pike fishing on this type of river is quite different from fishing stillwaters. Indeed many anglers I know have tried it and found the going hard. To the uninitiated, a river can be daunting. Rivers are obviously affected more quickly by changes in conditions than other waters. Rain is a major drawback; it only takes a few hours for the level to become unfishable, yet the best part of a week to clear and go down again. Another deterrent for most is loose floating weed and even in winter small amounts still drift down, and continually circle round in slacks and eddies. I could go on listing these so-called disadvantages, not least being of course the strength of the current itself, but to me these factors constitute the challenge and essence of river piking.

The main reason why most become disillusioned, however, is because they have failed to achieve results. On a lot of stillwaters fishing tends to be a communal affair and it may not take long to discover where the pike are and what the going method is. On rivers it is different. You are faced alone with mile upon mile of water totally deserted in the winter months. When I first moved to Hampshire, it took me a while to adapt and get used to solitary fishing, but now I would have it no other way. In fact, I am sure that it is one of the main factors contributing to my success. Talking to other anglers or a friend, although possibly serving a useful purpose, does tend to slow you down. Winter days are short and river piking entails a lot of non-fishing time, while you just move about.

A solitary angler is free to roam where he will and to move on at his own speed to a different swim or stretch of water. This is a vital factor. Keep mobile. There is no place here for your bivvies and bed chairs. Fishing with a friend also cuts your chances by half, as on any given stretch there may only be a few likely swims, thus you are both effectively fishing for the same fish. Is this selfish? Well, perhaps, but I feel it goes deeper than this. On your own you can concentrate and get a better feel for the river, and it definitely helps with the most important aspect of river piking – location.

Location

The most obvious swims are, of course, slacks. There is no doubt that pike do spend some of their time in slacks, so these are the most likely places to make a start. All rivers have their own individual characteristics and some are more 'pikey' looking than others. The Dorset Stour for example has far more slacks than the Hampshire Avon and, therefore, is a lot easier to pike fish. Every slack is worth trying, but it soon becomes obvious that there are slacks and there are slacks!

At the bottom of the scale there are those that rarely produce anything more than jacks, whilst others are a safe bet for double figure fish. Why should this be? One answer may be the quantity, and perhaps the quality, of available food, and this is where a good knowledge of other species inhabiting each stretch of river is invaluable. Find out what the roach fishing is like or if it is a good chub and dace length.

This 27lb fish encapsulates the beauty of Wessex piking.

Indeed, all the areas from which I have taken good pike produce specimen roach, plenty of pound plus shoal-sized chub as well as runs of sea trout.

If the local pleasure fishing grapevine does not extend as far as the stretch being considered, then the only way to find out about it is to spend time spotting in the summer, or actually to fish for other species. I tend to do the latter, not just to seek out pike food, but simply because I like fishing for other species if conditions are not entirely suited to pike. Obviously, knowledge gained in this way is very useful.

Unfortunately, locating a good slack is not always as simple as finding a good food supply. There are a lot of slacks which, despite having a good head of other species, rarely produce pike at all. It may be the geography of the area is not to the pikes' liking, although from the surface this may seem hard to believe. Depth is a factor worth considering. For some reason deep slacks are not usually productive. What to us may look ideal does not necessarily appeal to the pike. Anything approaching nine feet or more is, in my experience, not a good swim and I look for a depth of between two to eight feet.

Another relevant feature is some remaining weed growth or bankside rushes, which in their dead winter state tend to hang into the water and form a canopy over it. Overhanging bushes with perhaps an accompanying raft of flotsam caught up in the branches form another potential lurking spot.

Slacks frequented by a good head of big fish are usually not suited to smaller pike for obvious reasons. Here, maybe, is a reason why jacks congregate in other swims. However, the question remains why do these jack swims not attract the larger fish? The answer to this is still a mystery to me so, as I said earlier, every slack is worth a try as you approach a new stretch of river.

In general, however, most slacks that are good pike swims have a fair exchange of fish. Some days it will be all smallish fish, other days these will be absent and the odd good sized fish may be taken there. If, however, a couple of 'jack attacks' greet your baits in the first few minutes it is usually a bad sign. Give the swim a short while and then find the nearest piece of water that looks like a reasonable prey species swim and try again there. As I said earlier, if you have previous knowledge of such swims so much the better.

Not all river pike rely on slacks and their surroundings for their existence. If they did, rivers like the Hampshire Avon, where the number of slacks is low, would contain precious few pike. So, what other features do I look for? A slow curve is a good place to start. Most of the main push sweeps around the outside of a curve leaving slower, steadier water under the inside bank. A section of this nature is not so much a swim but an area of river which can be anything from fifteen to a hundred yards long and, therefore, needs searching out thoroughly.

Insides of curves are invariably shallow, either because they are slightly silted, or because the gravel has escaped the shifting power of floods. Dace are usually the main inhabitants, finding conditions to their liking and having somewhere to retreat to in times of high water. Remember dace shoals tend to move around a bit and consequently pike can just about be anywhere, following their prey.

I come now to my favourite type of swim which I call the 'under the bank swim'. This consists of a slower band of water under the bank, usually up to six or eight feet wide and caused by some upstream feature like a slightly protruding piece of bank, tree stump, or sudden widening of the river where the depth has not decreased. If it is in the range of four to six feet deep with an overhanging canopy of dead bankside foliage along its length, so much the better. Like the curve areas these swims can be of any length, and the longer they are the better chance there is of finding more than one fish. They are the sort of place that look like good roach and chub swims and they usually are, so pike are likely to be present as well. That feeling of anticipation as you work your way down them, fishing right under the rod top, is very hard to beat in piking.

Opposite *Dave Plummer prepares to unhook a thirty-two pounder for Tony Miles. Note that the fish is well protected by sacking.*

Tackle and technique

For various reasons long rods are really useful in rivers. I carry two around with me both twelve feet long. One is for wobbling and the other for various forms of live-baiting. Line takes a lot of punishment, constantly casting and retrieving, pulling out of weed and snags and battling through undergrowth. There is no point in taking chances especially fishing at close range with strong currents, so I never go lighter than fourteen or fifteen pounds B.S. A big fish hooked in these situations is a different animal altogether from one played in gradually from fifty yards on a stillwater.

Most stretches contain some interesting swims on both banks, so to avoid an extra walking distance I like to at least try and fish as many as I can from the same bank, usually by float paternostering. This may entail some accurate casting if the swim is only a small one and also cause consider-able arm ache. One has to stand and hold the rod as high as possible to keep the line off the water. At this distance it does not take much to shift the lead. A strong breeze or floating weed will do it, so do not be afraid of using a large bomb, three ounces if necessary. These river pike do not seem to mind dragging a lot of gear around once they have decided to take. If the line sags on to the main push of the river this again will cause the bait to lose position, so close concentration is essential. The use of smaller baits in this situation is helpful, making tackle control much easier.

All methods work in slacks, although there are times when one technique may be noticeably better than another. A float paternostered livebait may remain un-touched, while a free roving float fished livebait or a wobbled deadbait takes fish. Be flexible in your approach and do not assume that because one favoured method has failed they all will. However, I have found bottom fished deadbaits to be gener-ally nowhere near as effective as livebait or wobbling. This may be due to the types of weather conditions in which I like to fish, but I will elaborate on this later.

When fishing curves I find wobbling a deadbait the most effective method, not only because a greater area can be covered but because the depth is usually variable, shallowing up the closer in you fish to the inside of the curve. It is also the nicest way to fish this type of area – casting directly across and allowing the current to swing the bait around in an arc, until it is at an angle of about forty-five degrees to the bank. By this time it will be entering the slower water and should have sunk fairly close to the bottom. By raising the rod and, therefore, lifting the bait higher in the water, it can then be worked back in the usual fashion. I don't like to fish it too close to the bottom on the upstream retrieve, as I feel sneaking up from behind, on the same plain as a pike, is a bit unnatural in pre-sentation. I am not saying this will not work, but I prefer to pass the bait overhead rather than alongside fish-holding posi-tions in the current.

Deadbaits around the four ounce mark are an ideal size for wobbling on rivers. Mine are weighted with short lengths of mild steel bar (six millimetres in diameter). The lengths vary between one and a half and three and a half inches, depending on current strength and depth. Tie a six inch length of ten pound nylon around one end of the weight and then push the other end down the bait throat until the tied end is in its mouth. The top treble of a two treble trace is then passed through both lips and the two loose ends of nylon are tied around the shank. This means that even if the bait is lost the weight is returned. I prefer steel to barrel leads. If a bait is lost complete with weight I do not like the idea of the pike picking it up and possibly having a slow death from lead poisoning.

For weirpools, I dispense with the float

Bob Mousley's Weighted Deadbait Wobbling Rig

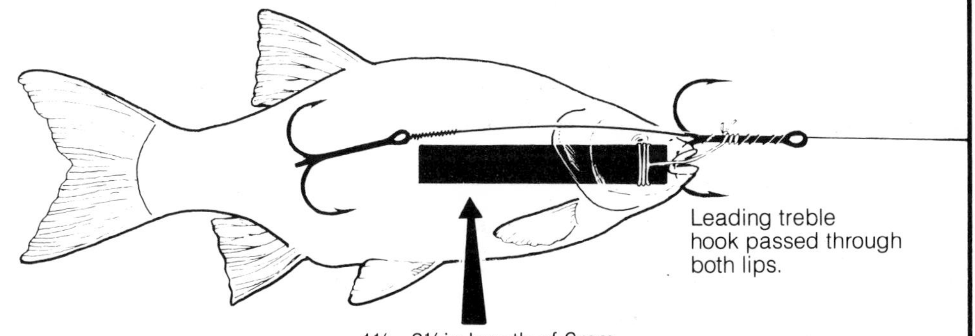

Leading treble
hook passed through
both lips.

1½–3½in length of 6mm
diameter mild steel
bar, pushed into throat
of bait and tied to shank
of the leading treble hook.

and simply straight paternoster livebaits, keeping the rod high to prevent the bait finding any possible snags such as discarded masonry from when the weir was built. A float creates far too much surface drag and is more a hindrance than a help.

For 'under the bank swims' a long rod really comes into its own, enabling you to keep back from the water's edge so that the tip just reaches over the marginal cover. In such swims two methods work well. Again float paternostered livebaits are one of my favourites but need a little more attention to detail. Firstly, use a slightly heavier bomb than is normally necessary to hold the bait in position. The reason for this is that when a bait becomes aware of a pike, it often gets a sudden shot of adrenalin and dives for the nearest cover, which in this case is very close by. The last thing you need is for the bait to become entangled at the crucial moment. Secondly, I use a short length of wire between the paternoster link

and the bait's nose, never more than a foot. Again this is to restrict the livebait's movement and prevent it from reaching cover. If the free length of trace is any longer, the bait tends to move all over the place.

Fish at about two-thirds depth, as there is no way of telling in this type of swim whether a pike is lying on the bottom a few feet out, or tucked right up under any available bankside cover. Start at the upstream end and gradually move down by lifting the bomb a few inches and walking four or five feet at a time downstream. Let it settle for a minute or two, then repeat the action until the whole length of the swim has been covered. Takes vary from a slow sinking of the float, to a full-blooded lunge across the surface, which never fails to take me by surprise even if I am half expecting it. I liken it to the feeling you get when a pheasant takes flight from cover just before you step on it.

The second method is float wobbling deadbait. This consists of using the same type of weighted deadbait as previously described, but with the addition of a float fixed top and bottom with rubbers and set just over depth. Start at the top of the swim and trot down holding back so that the bait wafts up slightly in the current. Release the hold completely once in a while and allow the bait to reach bottom. Then check the outflow of line altogether and pull back slightly so that the bait rises almost to the surface. This can be very effective and often induces a savage take. Once a trot has reached ten to fifteen yards, slowly retrieve as close to the bank as possible with the bait higher in the water. Streamline floats are useful for this method as they make less wake. Pike have been known to take a liking to fat-bodied surface-popping ones.

Conditions

I mentioned earlier about fishing for other species if conditions are not suited to pike. It has been my experience over the last few years that on the rivers I fish, pike become much more co-operative during cold weather. If the air temperature falls to a few degrees either side of freezing and stays there, I feel far more confident than if the weather is mild, when I often fish for other species. Our grandfathers must have had these rivers in mind when they applied their old maxim of having 'a good frost on the ground' before it is worth piking.

The arctic conditions at the beginning of 1982 were just about on the limit. I do not mean limits of self-endurance here, although roving about in such weather does have the effect of draining one's energy more rapidly than in clement conditions. No, I was still catching the occasional pike, it is just that I feared for their well-being while on the bank. I became aware of this just after dawn one morning with an air temperature of just sixteen degrees Fahrenheit and a water temperature of thirty-six degrees. An eighteen pound pike had chomped a really lively dace, and from banking to completion of unhooking and weighing only a minute or so must have passed. It was after this very short time that I noticed the fins had taken on a strange dry appearance. They were starting to freeze! After all, with a body temperature of thirty-six degrees Fahrenheit it won't take long with an air and ground temperature of sixteen degrees to lose just four degrees. With visions of hypothermia occurring, I hurriedly returned her to the relative warmth of the river without even having the opportunity to admire her lovely markings.

I know warmer winter periods usually mean rain with the obvious consequence of high, coloured water, but this is not always the case. On the majority of occasions when I have fished in theoretically ideal conditions – good water clarity, nice and mild – 'jack days' have been the norm. I am not saying that you will not catch at all and I have taken a few good fish at such times, but it is a much more unpredictable affair – odd fish rather than the more consistent results of fishing in colder weather.

A possible reason for poor results could be that at the start of a mild spell, with a few degrees rise in temperature and subsequent appetite stimulation, the pike have quickly had their fill and, therefore, are not really interested in taking anything more. Remember, unlike stillwaters, a pike has only to move a short distance in such a river to find good enough quality food. Preoccupation with fry feeding, a common occurrence on stillwaters, is unknown on the rivers I fish.

Opposite *Bob Mousley with a huge bag of Wessex river fish which included two twenty pounders.*

A double slides in towards the snow-clad river bank. River pike keep feeding, however low the temperature.

A last important factor, in my view, is the type of bait that is successful in cold weather. You can almost imagine several pike lying practically motionless in the icy water, apart from stabilising fin movements in the current, perhaps not having fed for a few days. Other species in the vicinity are probably doing the same thing. If it is cold, working a really lively bait to a swim seems to galvanise what I believe are not feeding pike into action. Suddenly, this flashing, struggling fish comes on the scene, proving too much for an instantly awakened predatory instinct to resist.

All I can add further is a dislike for bright sunny days. Then, there is always a chance of a fish or two first thing, but there is a long wait until late afternoon and evening. Cold overcast days, good water clarity and the river at a reasonable level give me the best overall chance of catching several good fish from the type of swims I mentioned earlier. These are the days I would be nowhere else but on the Wessex rivers.

A NEW RIVER WAVENEY RECORD

Some while ago M.P. was part of a campaign on the lower Waveney, the large East Anglian river. His partner, Dave Humphries, caught the record for that river, and this is M.P.'s retelling of the capture.

Did we ever get to know the lower Waveney? This is a question I cannot answer and which haunts me even now at times. Certainly, we learnt from our sessions on the river. We began to understand her moods, her ways, and as time passed we began to catch more and more of her fish, yet still I am uncertain. She was capricious, like a woman, and our time spent with her was really no more than an apprenticeship. It would take a decade to understand that river completely, and to develop real intimacy, if indeed such a knowledge is at all possible.

We were so naive during those first few sessions on the water, expecting pike to lie in all the textbook places. But this was a unique river. She was so deep, permanently coloured and possessed with a tidal influence that could even dislodge our twenty-eight pound anchors at times. Her moods were violent and where one minute an ebb tide raged, suddenly all would be still, only to be followed less than a minute later by a raging flood tide. She was a man's water to whom, as the uninitiated, we had to prove ourselves.

All the same, problems make for interesting fishing and we certainly had no intention of being defeated. We increased the amount of weight we used, varied the methods and experimented in every way

we knew, to please her. Soon we were no longer faced with paternosters uncontrollably bouncing along the bottom, or even being lifted from the bottom altogether in the strong surging current. We mastered ways of laying herrings on the bottom, upstream against the tide. There was no place for trolling on this water as it would have been almost impossible to control the boat against the tide, and anyway it was too heavily coloured for the method to work well. This was a water which required a slow search, swim by swim, using paternostered livebaits and deadbaits on the bottom. By applying logic and sense, we soon fished relatively unperturbed by these

Charlie Beane with a 22lb 3oz pike from the Waveney.

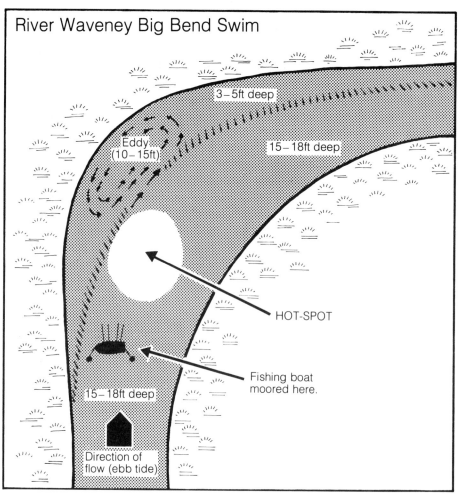

River Waveney Big Bend Swim

3–5ft deep

Eddy (10–15ft)

15–18ft deep

HOT-SPOT

Fishing boat moored here.

15–18ft deep

Direction of flow (ebb tide)

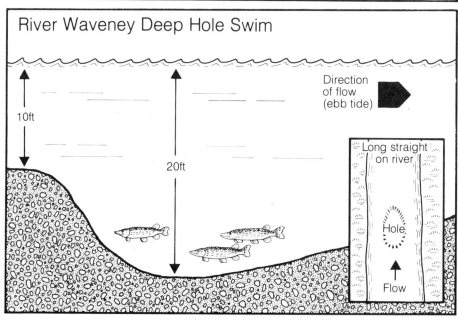

River Waveney Deep Hole Swim

Direction of flow (ebb tide)

10ft

20ft

Long straight on river

Hole

Flow

conditions which were so different from our usual Norfolk Broads and rivers.

As you would expect, we found that certain times or, more relevantly, certain tides produced the greatest sport. Very few fish came except at the turn of the tide or when there was a strong seaward flow. We found also that our paternostered baits needed to be anchored by two or even three ounce weights, and that livebaits fished in this way were very effective despite the water colour. On location we soon discovered that the important question was what *was* happening, as opposed to what *appeared* to be happening, under the surface. It seemed that in many circumstances the bends were not holding areas. Perhaps the flow changing with the tides was too unsettling in

Dave Humphries shows a last glimpse of his record-breaking Waveney pike.

these places. Certainly long straights between two bends brought more returns.

Only on the big slow bends, where 'proper' slacks could be found, were results forthcoming. In retrospect we should have used an echo-sounder to find those unnoticed and inexplicable depth changes which occurred along the bottom. These were the places to seek out, the edges of these drop-offs, which seemed to be ideal ambush spots for the pike.

Much remained a mystery. Why, despite abundant food supplies, did the pike eat so many eels, or why did they prefer mackerel to herrings? We never did learn why they moved or when, or to where, and where from. All we found were a few productive swims, and we fished these on good and bad days. These swims always seemed to hold one or two reasonable fish, but they were always different fish. They were

holding, resting areas, dovetailing with the nomadic lifestyle of these wandering pike.

Then on one morning, no different from the rest, we anchored in one of our more productive areas, a great slow bend with a true gully running alongside the slack. Our two livebaits were cast downstream of the boat, fished on the long paternostered tails which we had found to be most effective. Four foot tails kept the bait well off the bottom in fifteen to eighteen feet of water. The tide that morning had been ebbing strongly for several hours, and the surface boiled in our swim, despite its great depth.

We found as usual we did not have too long to wait and I soon had a run from a small fish. The next run of the day was Dave's, typical of a big Waveney pike. It hit his bait and simply steamed off. This was no half-hearted jack take. The line left the reel at the speed of a belting carp. Dave had no need to strike, and the mere action of engaging the bale arm was enough to hammer in the hooks.

The rod bent in his hands under the speed of the fish. Then there was the first fighting run, of a power seemingly borrowed from a giant catfish. Eventually she stopped and from then it was only a question of time and hard pumping to ease an obviously large pike back against the flow. Minutes later she surfaced, from the deeps, a good twenty certainly, we knew, and Dave's personal best. She was bigger than that though, a previously uncaught beauty, and as well-nourished as any pike I have ever seen. She was a river thirty by an ounce, the record for the water.

That fish also proved to be the end of fishing for us that day, though we did try to fish on, but we had achieved our goal – a gigantic fast water pike and that was enough. So we eased the boat to the bank, photographed and released Dave's prize and then he produced a hip flask of brandy, saved for this very occasion.

Large Stillwaters

It could seem wrong at first sight, to class all stillwaters together. For instance, the shallow estate lake when compared to the vast expanses of Abberton Reservoir may seem very different. When analysed, however, are there so many real distinctions?

It is true that the shallow lake may not lend itself to sophisticated trolling techniques with lead core line, but trolling itself can still be exceedingly successful on shallow water. The concept is the same, it is just that the tackle has to be different to overcome the problems of deep water trolling.

The drop-offs also may not be present at first examination but then in shallow water a one foot depth change is, relatively speaking, a very significant drop-off. It is for reasons such as these that we have grouped stillwaters together, for although there are differences in water type, and these become more obvious during the course of this section, there are in fact many more similarities.

For the majority of pike anglers, fishing centres around stillwaters and a review over the last ten years suggests that the average stillwater pike angler has become very stereotyped in his approach. There have been small advances in bite indication systems with the drop-off indicators, for example, but a uniformity of bait and method seems to have arisen, which for many is difficult to break. Countless pike anglers arrive at their destination and proceed to send two deadbaits the statutory sixty yards into the lake and then the rods are placed on rests for hour upon hour, waiting for the pike to arrive.

This approach was initially developed for the correct reasons and applied to those circumstances, where the pike were becoming wary of venturing close to the bank on well-fished waters. As competition on these stillwaters increased and all the pike anglers began to send baits to the same distant position, we ended up with a situation where the pike ventured everywhere except that sixty yard band that runs parallel to the accessible bank.

It does appear, however, that an awakening is beginning! Possibly men such as Eddie Turner, Bill Hancock, Vic Gibson and others of the drifting vein, have helped this by bringing a more versatile approach to the public. More and more we foresee anglers experimenting with their methods and, in so doing, beginning to change their approach on large stillwaters. There still will, of course, be a place for the legered and float fished deadbait which, when used thoughtfully, will often produce large pike. There will also be those who continue to wait hour upon hour with their long range deadbaits and through persistence they will continue to catch fish, but at the same time they will miss some of the enjoyment which can be achieved by a more versatile approach.

As trends on these waters change, and as the competition increases, the more searching techniques will reveal more of the potential of some of our larger still-waters. We personally consider that the home of the English pike record will not remain at a Norfolk Broadland water but will ultimately settle at one of the many trout reservoirs and lakes throughout the country.

Pits and reservoirs in particular are likely to form the basis of future generations' pike fishing as our rivers suffer from pollution and abstraction and our broads and estate lakes diminish through silting. As a result we foresee a continual increase in the number of waters specifically developed as pike fisheries. Reality dictates that, although one may prefer 'virgin' waters, as more leisure time becomes available and consequently there are more anglers and pike fishermen, there will be a greater demand for more stillwater pike fisheries and ultimately such waters will become commercial propositions. These waters will fulfil a need but, unless managed very carefully, are unlikely to be waters from which very large pike are taken.

Increased competition and the resulting more efficient breed of pike angler brings a further problem – increased pressure on fish which can suffer badly during capture, especially in inexperienced hands. As a result, fishery management may also become vital in order to maintain our pike stocks.

In the short term, therefore, we would expect some extremely large fish to be caught in our larger stillwaters, but in the very long term, sadly, we expect that the future of English pike fishing may settle with managed fisheries, with very few unpiked waters remaining.

THE DRIFTING TECHNIQUE

We met Eddie Turner and Bill Hancock by a vast inland fishery on a day at the tail end of the January freeze-up. The wind was sharp, with rain turning to sleet that did little to melt the great ice floes that were drifting over the lake. Throughout that day very little was caught. I remember two doubles taken, and a low twenty was landed before Martyn and I arrived. Hour after hour we all sat in cars by the bankside, talking, swapping flasks, making occasional dashes out to the rods. Eddie and Bill were prepared, but then they are experienced men. At 1 p.m. the smell of freshly fried beefburgers came from the back of Eddie's estate, was caught in the wind and swirled along the bankside.

It was the kind of day that shows just how foolish it is to skimp on warm winter clothing. The only men who could stick that weather out were those thermalised and waterproofed from head to toe. You cannot fish if you are uncomfortable. Before very long you realise fishing is never compulsory and you are on your way home.

Eddie and Bill are the best type of company on such a day. A mass of stories, a fund of good advice and intriguing ideas, they are both modern-thinking anglers and this comes over in minutes. Both men are positive in everything they do. They are never still in either body or brain – they are two live wires against the cold. Both men have great belief in big stillwaters for pike. They do not deny that smaller waters can, and often do, produce the occasional large fish, but they feel that the potential of the great reservoirs and vast pit systems is all but unlimited. It is this aspect that obviously excites them both – the knowledge that they could be on to monster thirty pound plus fish. Certainly, their list of fish up to thirty-three pounds plus backs up this faith.

Large waters are rarely overfished and this is vital. To grow really massive, pike need sanctuary from anglers, and this is what waters of more than a hundred acres offer, especially if boats are not allowed out. Also, these inland seas discourage

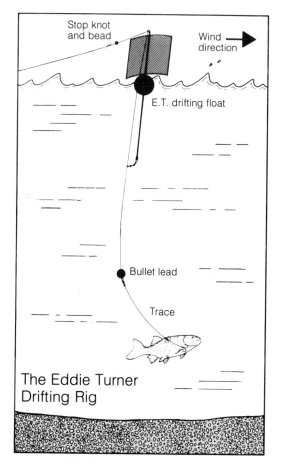

The Eddie Turner Drifting Rig

many fishermen who simply lack the confidence to tackle anywhere so huge. Serious winter piking on these waters is not for anyone but experts, or at least, people who do more than chuck and chance a bait.

Another reason for their confidence in big stillwaters is the fact that all species of fish in many of these greater reservoirs, pits and lakes grow large, not just the pike. Record roach, bream and tench, and huge carp and chub come from these places. They have the capacity to produce exceptional fish, and they do so to the dedicated – the men with steady purpose and carefully laid plans.

There is a last factor that appeals to Eddie and Bill – big waters demand from them a positive attitude. They give scope for their inventiveness. Even on the foul day we were with them, the effort continued. They were not happy to sit back, bivvied and calm, comatose behind their drop-offs or buzzers. They like to cover water, they want to work at their fishing. They are busy men with little fishing time which they want to use to the utmost. To do this, they need to search a water.

First of all they are prepared to travel. On a big stillwater, they firmly believe it is necessary to be mobile – theirs is not a lazy man's sport. They go prepared for mile long walks; their accessories go in light rucksacks, their rods are made up, baits are carried in small buckets. They firmly believe that just as the accessible spots are often the worst fishing places, so the inaccessible areas are frequently the best. Almost certainly, however, it is their development of the drifting method that has made them famous today. It is in the drifting technique that they put so much faith to search out a big water – their slogan is to 'drift and find'. The drift is their key to success.

Here we must say that propelling, or casting, or in any way getting bait long distances to pike has for a long time been a preoccupation with serious anglers. We were first aware of it in the modern angling generation, in Frank Guttfield's first, well-loved book *In Search of Big Fish*, where he describes efforts to get pike baits to a sunken forest a great distance from the bank. Remote-controlled, motorised boats have been, and are still being used to get terminal gear out long distances. This is a controversial and expensive method, often criticised as it can disturb other people's fishing, and importantly, a boat takes the baits over the heads of fish close to the bank. 'Ballooning' has long been practised. The balloon, attached to a float or a trace, will catch the wind and carry tackle immense distances at very quick rates.

Eddie and Bill are quick to admit that their drifting techniques are an extension of other people's ideas but, with their ingenuity, they have built upon old theories to produce a rig that does work and has caught some very big fish for them, and for many others, including J.B.

The need to get baits out a long way on large stillwaters where a boat could not be used became apparent to Eddie and Bill the second season they tackled Star Tops, one of the large reservoirs in the Tring group. The first year, they were very successful, but the second year their results plummeted. Both men knew that the fish were in the water, and suspected they had moved out of casting range, into inaccessible water.

Here then, in Hertfordshire, the experiment began. On each visit they took float-building equipment with them as a travelling kit of different stems, float vanes and buoyancy balls. They took a selection of glues to try out on the bankside. Gradually

Opposite This 30lb pike proves that the drifter does work. The tape measure is a sign that more and more pike men are becoming concerned with the statistics of big fish.

Roger Miller holds a finely marked lower twenty which came to a smelt deadbait.

the prototypes improved and, as the baits got further and further from the bank, results picked up as well. One day they took five doubles. On another two doubles and a twenty-four pounder, and they were well on the road to success. Both men admit that the drifting float now available is not yet the perfected article and they are still improving on it, but we have now at our disposal a method that adds a whole new dimension to big stillwater fishing.

Possibly, one of the main delights of drifting is that it makes stillwater piking a more enjoyable pastime. Drifting is a method that demands a certain amount of thought and activity, not unlike long trotting on a river. The half-dead, bivvied angler behind his bobbins is not the drifting man. Personally we feel a tremendous excitement when we know our baits are covering unfished, or at least very lightly

fished water. The numbing boredom of much winter deadbait piking is transformed. Areas we have always had feelings for can be worked. We know we're not leaving any stones unturned or, in this case, pike uncovered.

More vitally, drifting does catch pike when other methods fail. There is nothing now to stop the whole of big waters being covered by the positive pike angler, unless one or more banks are inaccessible. Eddie and Bill reckon their maximum effective drifting range is 250 yards or more, so to have two, three or four rods on the go like this is to cover a tremendous area of water each hour. In fact, we guess that the area each bait covers is approximately one acre of water.

So, if drifting can get past the limits of ordinary casting range to less suspicious pike, it can also be used as a method to search out long range holding areas. Features to investigate with the drifter are numerous: trees fallen into the water; any known gullies, ledges or deeper areas;

islands and the entrances of rivers and streams; culverts, pumping stations, trout cages, boathouses and lily or weed beds. Flooded hedges and drowned woodlands are also past success areas. Shoals of fry dimpling the surface can be drifted too, and both men agree it pays to concentrate on areas where the bait fish are seen or caught from.

Vic Gibson shows how to release a large pike, supporting it vertically until it gathers strength to move off.

Eddie and Bill recommend the areas off the eastern banks of gravel pits in particular. Considering our prevailing winds are southerlies and westerlies, a lot of food tends to drift into the north-eastern corner of pits, large lakes and reservoirs. There too the winds and currents create a scouring action, that can produce deeper water than elsewhere. So, easterly winds can be used to drift out from the east bank, just as westerlies will send a bait towards it. The only time the drifting man is really caught out is when there is no wind at all.

One particular advantage the drifter gains is to reach pike that are lying up outside their hunting areas nearer the bank. We were given a particular example of a large lake where the food fish tended to stay close in shore. At feeding times, the pike came in for them, but then perhaps not long after dawn, drifted out of normal range once more. With the drifter the pike could be reached and, though they were not actively on the prowl, they would pick off fish that came to them. They were lazy pike but not against feeding if the right opportunity presented itself. In this way, the drifting method prolonged the taking hours and extended the whole sport of the day.

On its way, a drifter covers all the water to its maximum range, from the start of a short fifteen to twenty yard cast, to a distance of over two hundred yards. Pike anywhere along this route can be taken. With long casting techniques capable of reaching eighty to a hundred yards, the water between the bank and the point of bait entry will have gone unfished, and pike in the margin will be passed over. Both anglers stressed that the margins are hot areas, and Bill in particular, praised the second shelf in gravel pits as a very productive area which is often cast over. The drifter does not do this. It fishes from where it goes in, to where it finishes.

A drifting man likes all the usual pike weather, but he does need a wind. A perfect strength is force three or four, a steady wind that gives a decent ripple and pushes the drifter out nicely. If the wind is slight and the ripple begins a long way from the bank, a balloon can help get the bait out to the working area. A strong wind, say force six or more, causes its own problems. Frequently the waves are so high that a float with a very large drifting vane has to be used, simply to be seen at distances through the spray. And of course this increases the speed of the

already fast drift, and probably takes a bait too quickly over a pike's head. It would seem that a small vane float would be better but this would be all but invisible at a hundred and fifty plus yards, and a pike could be deep hooked. The answer is a large vaned visible float, carefully held back to travel more slowly than the currents.

Like so many good pike men, Eddie and Bill stress the importance of their baits. They must have confidence in them to fish well. Without the baits they want they would not go fishing. It is quite as simple as that.

They are definite about the best baits for drifting. They want good-sized livebaits, not massive but they must be a decent meal for a big pike. We both agree with Eddie and Bill over this point. For a large pike to follow and attack a moving bait requires effort, and the result of this effort must be worthwhile. A big predator will not chase a small bait. It is not worth the effort it expends and the drift will go over unsuccessfully. Small livebaits are far better paternostered, pretty well static close to a pike which can then make up its mind at leisure, and take it with little energy loss. There are, of course, exceptions, but we are talking about putting good pike on the bank consistently.

Where trout are available as livebaits, we believe they would be excellent. They are the right size at about six or seven ounces. They are extremely tough, and work well for long periods, and it is this tirelessness that after a short while can drive a pike into a strike. Trout can quite literally drive a pike wild until they take out of spite, out of fury, out of a quite wicked malevolence. Buying trout for bait has an added advantage for us all. Unpleasant as it may seem, they are born to be killed and the natural

Opposite *This enormous 33lb 4oz fish fell to Eddie Turner from a large stillwater.*

born fish of our waters are left unmolested. Pike men in these later years of this century must be conservationists to a great extent, and the roach and dace stocks of our rivers especially are alarmingly depleted in many lowland areas. Livebaiting is an issue that none of us can now afford to ignore.

Whilst livebaits are their favourites, Eddie and Bill still use deadbaits on the drift with confidence. Any normal fish baits can be fished well when mounted horizontally and at times have out-fished livebaits, even when the two have been close together. Perhaps a pike sees a deadbait as representing more meat for less effort, especially as the drifting method imparts just that little extra attractive life to it.

Baits should ideally be fished approximately two feet from the bottom. Eddie and Bill prefer depths up to twenty feet and not much below. Of course there are problems especially in pits which can have very variable bottom contours, with shallow bars either side of deep gullies. Eddie and Bill experiment all the time with depths. This takes us back to the joys of drifting. It is mind rather than mindless fishing. They build up a good overall impression of the water they are tackling and set their drifting floats as close to the optimum depths as they can.

The pike takes the bait. It could happen close in, but more likely the great event will be at one, two or even nearer three hundred yards. Perhaps the drifter float sinks. This is easy but it could travel up wind, or simply stop in its tracks. Again the message is to be alert. Any untoward movement must be wound down and checked. Nobody wants a deep hooked pike. Binoculars help give a close up scrutiny of the float movements, but at all costs, both men demand that we should strike as soon as we suspect a take has developed. By the time we have seen the float indication, and then wound down

tight, the bait could have been turned.

You do not strike at two hundred yards. You tighten down, perhaps walk backwards, rod held high. The hook is pulled home, not so much by your efforts, as by the weight of the fish itself bending its head into the trebles. Jacks often bounce themselves off. Not so the big fish whose bulk betrays them at this vital movement.

Eddie and Bill have developed a super rig for hooking fish at extreme range. Its effectiveness depends on the flying treble hanging free over the back of the bait, which can find a hook hold in the pike's mouth without having to break free of the bait first. M.P. has used this rig to great effect.

With a fish on, it is essential never to give it slack line. At colossal range there is little pressure on the hooks to keep them in the pike's mouth, and it is vital to keep on what pressure there is.

Drifting demands a lot of the tackle. A rod should be as long and as light as possible. The length is for good line control, for lifting the belly of the water as it develops, and for extra speed in tightening to the pike on the take. Lightness is also essential because this is almost the matchmen way of pike fishing. You will be holding the rod a great deal of the time, rather than watching it doze in its rests. Carbon, therefore, is a first choice. The Tri-Cast twelve foot two and a half pound test curve rod is superb. Reels are also important. The spool must be big enough to accommodate at least two hundred and fifty yards of line. Eddie and Bill both use large Cardinal 57s and here it is important to remember that a metal spool should be used. There is immense pressure loaded on to a reel when winching in a big fish from a distance, a pressure so great that it can shatter a plastic spool. This creates tangle and invariably means a lost pike.

Lines should have eleven or twelve pounds breaking strain. Maxima is excel-

Eddie Turner's Super Rig

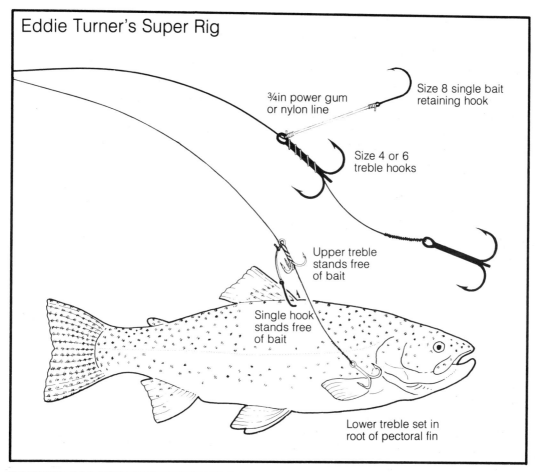

¾in power gum
or nylon line

Size 8 single bait
retaining hook

Size 4 or 6
treble hooks

Upper treble
stands free
of bait

Single hook
stands free
of bait

Lower treble set in
root of pectoral fin

The Eddie Turner Autogreaser

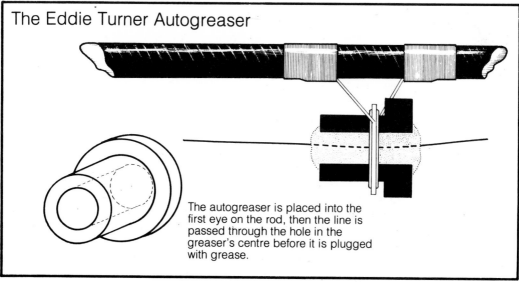

The autogreaser is placed into the
first eye on the rod, then the line is
passed through the hole in the
greaser's centre before it is plugged
with grease.

lent as it stretches less than many of its rivals, an obvious advantage when it comes to keeping pressure on at colossal range. Another make, Sylcast, is a very tough line, however, and Bill in particular recommends this. Most essential, however, is to check line very carefully, especially if you suspect it has been over the top of a shallow gravel bar, and has perhaps been frayed in the process. It is essential that the line must float. For this reason, Eddie and Bill introduced the auto-greaser. This invention is typical of the two of them. They are always thinking, always trying to be one step ahead.

What is definite is that drifting has massively extended our range and versatility on large stillwaters. What is also very sure is that as more and more anglers realise its potential the method will not stand still. Eddie and Bill are already experimenting with better floats to improve presentation

Unhooking a big fish requires a firm hold, with the hand positioned under the gill flaps.

and be more easily manoeuvrable. Anybody who uses the method will have, or should have, his own ideas. The essence of the method lies with the thinking pike angler.

The float itself, for instance, will probably be modified. A wedge-shaped vane makes its way through the wind more efficiently and does not spin like the single-vaned float is prone to do. Eddie and Bill are already working on a prototype. There will be experimentation on the stem of the float itself, which will probably become fibreglass. We feel that this material will not bend like the present metal stems and will not shatter at range. This, we admit, is a theory but the potential is there if you are willing to explore it. There is even scope for development in the idea of underwater rudders, to allow the rig to steer across the wind, instead of merely following before it.

One of the weaknesses of the present drifter is in the top attachment, and unquestionably a new form of attachment will be found. Alternatively the top attach-

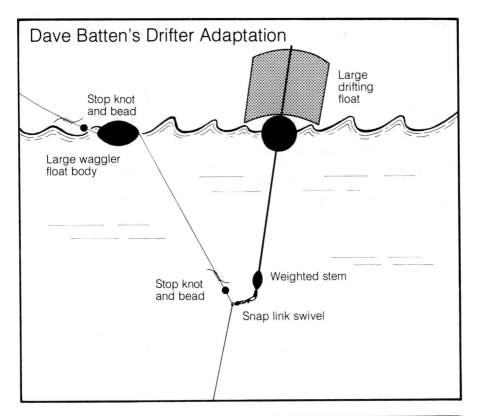

Dave Batten's Drifter Adaptation

Stop knot and bead

Large drifting float

Large waggler float body

Stop knot and bead

Weighted stem

Snap link swivel

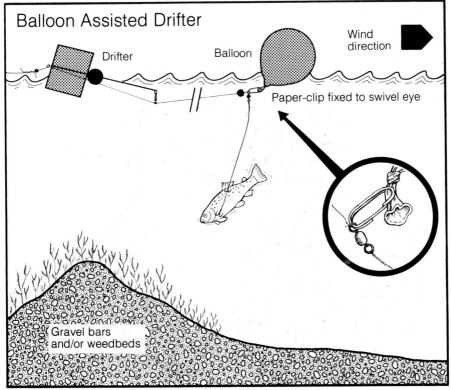

Balloon Assisted Drifter

Drifter

Balloon

Wind direction

Paper-clip fixed to swivel eye

Gravel bars and/or weedbeds

ment may be eliminated altogether. For example, Dave Batten, a Norwich angler, uses his own drifting float not attached at the top at all – he uses a balsa waggler body running loose on the line. This has advantages. It still folds back on the strike but the angler can cast it further without fear of the top attachment coming loose. The balsa body also helps the line float.

At times the drifter is criticised for being slow in getting to where the fish are. Indeed it is frustrating to catch a fish at long range, know a pike pack hangs there, but have to wait several minutes to return a bait to the hot area. By using a balloon in conjunction with a drifter the rig can be speeded to the area; the balloon is then struck off and the bait drifts through at a slower pace (see diagram above). Other advantages are that you can get over shallow and weedy areas to the deeper water and drift from there, and also take the float from sheltered areas in the lee of the bank that much quicker to the ripple.

16 A double figure river fish struggles
in the sub-zero temperatures of early
morning.

17 Above *Mick Brown holds a near-twenty weirpool pike that fell to a Hi-Low lure.*

18 Below *Pike! The head of a twenty-three pounder.*

19 Above *The reeds along the River Waveney shimmer with deep winter frost.*

20 Right *The end of a day for a river piker.*

21 Left *Eddie Turner supports pike of 27lb and 25lb.*

22 Below *Bob Mousley, well-wrapped against the weather, holds a lovely fish to the bright winter light.*

23 Opposite (top) *Bob Mousley returns a fine fish of 20lb 15oz, taken on a float paternostered livebait in the afternoon.*

24 Opposite (bottom) *This trout-water pike of 25lb 6oz fell to Mick Brown. It was 44in long, proving that not all trout-feeding pike are bulky fish.*

25 Above *Action in the early morning.*

26 Left *Steve Harper, a dedicated boat fisherman, holds a twenty-five pounder which fell to a trolled livebait.*

27 Above *Martyn Page holds a 24lb 14oz fish caught on a herring from a Bure broad.*

28 Below *Steve Harper cradles a Broadland thirty pounder.*

29 At 41lb 6oz, one of the biggest
British pike ever fully authenticated
fell to Neville Fickling in the early
months of 1985.

RESERVOIRS, GRAVEL PITS AND LARGE LAKES

by Vic Bellars

Eddie Turner and Bill Hancock have already given us an excellent way of exploring large waters using the drifting float. Vic Bellars looks at such places in even greater depth. He provides valuable insights into location and the nature of large stillwater pike.

As well as the difficulties normally encountered when tackling large waters, all too often others are imposed on anglers by riparian owners, or those who administer the fishery. Apart from certain reservoirs or gravel pits stocked as trout waters, or those used by sailing and ski clubs, boats are frequently prohibited. Even where boats are allowed on pits and lakes, the angler may be restricted to the use of oars only, power being disallowed. With the non-pollutant, silent electric outboards which are ideal for surveying and fishing large waters now available, I can think of no valid reasons to impose restrictions upon this form of propulsion. However, the no power rule often seems inviolate. If these further restrictions were not enough, some waters have 'no-go' areas, usually water-fowl reserves which boats may not enter. Even where only bank fishing is allowed, anglers can be restricted, being confined to certain areas, often poor in pike potential.

The pike angler is faced with further complications, for while one reservoir, pit or lake may appear similar to its counterpart, this is rarely so. Pike have different behaviour and feeding patterns, and may react differently to weather variations and wind directions from water to water. Each water should be considered unique. The reason for this is owed to many factors such as the geographical location of the fishery and the water quality, whether acid, neutral or alkaline, clear or coloured. The type of soil, subsoil and underlying rock determines water quality. Water quality will also depend on whether the water is stream, spring-fed or land-locked. Some waters will be open to the elements, others partially or fully sheltered by vegetation. The latter will have the nature of the bottom affected by detritus and be subject to freezing more easily than a water which is windswept. It is only possible to generalise about the three varieties of water covered in this section. Therefore each reservoir, pit or lake will be treated as typical of its type.

Reservoirs are normally much larger expanses of water, and pose problems not encountered to the same extent by gravel pits and lakes. Much of the main body of water will be a great depth, averaging thirty feet with even deeper areas. The deepest water will be off the dam wall, the shallowest at the opposite end to the dam and in the bays and arms. If the reservoir was formed by damming a river, the original river bed will remain as a trench, perhaps joined by subsidiary trenches, dykes and streams

Sharon Bailey plays a summer plug-hooked pike.

more shallow than the aforementioned waters. If a lake were formed by damming a stream, the underwater topography would be like a reservoir's, deeper at the dam end and, if stream-fed from the opposite end of the dam, extensive shallows will extend into the lake due to the deposited silt. The nature of the lake bed will differ from other waters, in that it will almost certainly be composed of soft mud formed by silt rotting down year after year. This will have some bearing on the best way to present bottom fish deadbaits that could easily sink in the layer of ooze.

All waters, as they mature, and as bankside vegetation increases, will become colonised by marginal plants. Flags, reed mace, mud sedges and Norfolk reeds are some of the more common varieties. Likewise in water of suitable depth, soft weed as well as narrow and broad-leaved lilies will proliferate. Knowing the position and type of aquatic vegetation is important, for fish visit these areas for food, spawning and cover. Such areas are naturally attractive to pike, as an easy source of food as well as lies for themselves.

Types of stillwater pike

Stillwater pike exhibit very different behavioural traits. Even within the confines of one water, not all the pike will behave in the same manner, but can be grouped as follows: some are dependent on one large shoal of prey, others are nomadic, more like foraging hunters, and the third group are those that remain largely territorial and rarely stray from their accustomed lies.

As a generalisation, nomadic pike are more likely to be encountered in reservoirs and gravel pits, the other categories being found in all three types of water. Obviously, nomadic pike are the most difficult to locate, for except when dormant while digesting food, they will be on the move. Furthermore, hunting pike will swim at the

that once fed the river before inundation.

Large gravel pits can also contain areas of great depth, but due to the gravel extraction process by which they were formed, there are many more variations in depths than in reservoirs. The pit bottom will be uneven, and may well consist of a series of sub-surface parallel bars, although the odd bar left higher than the rest may form an island. The bars will be separated by trenches of varying depth. Perhaps an apt description of a bed of a gravel pit would be that it is corrugated.

Lowland lakes are generally older and

same depth as their prey, which will not always, as is usually believed, be close to the bottom. Nomadic pike may well be encountered in the depth range from surface to mid-water. In pits, usually of lesser depth than reservoirs, and with greater bottom irregularities, hunting pike will establish more definable patrol routes. They will move through trenches, along the base of drop-offs, where a sloping ledge levels off and around islands. By such features, prey fish will congregate as any self-respecting pike well knows.

Even nomadic pike can be further subdivided into behaviour groups. Some will lie up by any convenient feature to digest food, the locality varying according to where the last meal was acquired. Others will set off on feeding patrols, only to return to a favoured holt, often some distance from the hunting areas.

Territorial pike are an enigma, apart from moving off to spawn, they will remain in the same spot year after year. While such fish may lie in any depth of water, some will remain in surprisingly shallow areas, even in the depths of winter. So they stay on, although the fish they prey on have departed to deeper water and, apart from the odd water-fowl or vole foolish enough to pass close by, no food is readily available.

Just as strange is that these fish, often very large indeed, choose an area to lie which seems devoid of any features normally considered attractive for pike to hole up in. It is only possible to surmise how these fish survive without loss of condition. Perhaps they do obtain enough nourishment from taking the odd water-fowl, but I tend to the theory that the metabolism of such fish changes to such an extent that they exist in a state of semi-hibernation.

I can offer no advice on how to discover the whereabouts of these isolated pike, but I do know that they will take a bait provided it is placed very close to them. I would expect to encounter these dormant fish in lakes and pits rather than in reservoirs.

Lastly, there are some pike that are territorial in that they will always be found in some favoured lie, or at least within the confines of a small localised area. These fish continue to feed throughout the year, and like the majority their greatest food intake will be in May and June. Thereafter it diminishes monthly until feeding ceases altogether during spawning. Such pike, though strongly territorial will move to a bait, and certainly choose lies from where they can ambush their prey.

While pike are not a shoal fish in the accepted sense, they do congregate at times in a very small area. This grouping can occur in any type of water. Why pike select a particular area to group like this is unknown to us, the anglers. These hot-spots can exist without any recognisable pike holding features to give any reasonable explanation as to why they have been chosen. These pike concentrations, until recently, could only have been discovered by chance, but with the increasing use of graph recorders such areas will be identifiable.

Holding areas and patrol routes

RESERVOIRS

In lowland reservoirs a large area of the bottom will be even, likened to a plateau, with a gradual increase in depth towards the dam end. Both at the dam end and at the sides there will be a positive change of inclination where the plateau and the base of the sloping sides meet. Fish tend to move along such a feature, also with the advantage of partial cover, at least to one side, pike can ambush a passing shoal of prey fish. Other pike will remain further out on the plateau, utilising a patch of stones or debris from which they can attack prey passing along the same route.

The bed of a reservoir will naturally

conform to the original land contours before inundation, unless the water has been long established. Therefore it is worthwhile seeking out an old Ordnance Survey map, as it could show holding areas in plenty. Apart from old river courses that have already been mentioned, there may well be the remains of isolated trees, thickets or spinneys, besides hedgerows, lanes, partly demolished buildings or those that have decayed into piles of rubble. All are potential fish holding areas and can be seen on an original map of the area.

The area surrounding valve towers seem attractive to fish, and the pipelines lying along the bottom that connect one valve to another and to the pumping station are certain pike holding features. If the reservoir is a trout fishery, the area adjacent to the stock cages will be a certain hot-spot. Any stream entering the reservoir, often through a culvert, will attract hordes of small fish which naturally attract pike, stationed just beyond the area where the current from the culvert slackens and dies away.

Apart from the features already mentioned any minor variation in the flatness of the bottom, for instance, a bed of pea mussels, a slight indentation, a hump or a tiny ledge, must be considered as a possible pike holding spot. Such unlikely and insignificant changes in contour can be quite as important as the more obvious ones, and such seemingly unimportant features attract both prey and predator. Lastly, the deep water of the dam is always worth fishing, whatever the nature of the bottom, and if the dam wall faces the prevailing wind, so much the better.

GRAVEL PITS

A gravel pit can be featureless, a bleak windswept sheet of water likened to a vast bowl in the countryside. Another can be a joy to behold, irregular in shape, dotted with tree laden islands, girt with marginal vegetation and even composed of a number of areas connected by channels or narrows. Scenic beauty is alas no indication of a good pike water. The former depressing waste may not only contain large fish of other species, but pike of impressive proportions as well.

Whatever the type of pit, the bottom configuration will be far more uneven than that of a reservoir. Depressions, bars, troughs and channels will occur, often within the compass of a relatively small area. Less natural features can be present, often in the shape of submerged gravel working machinery, and almost certainly the bottom will hold its share of old bedsteads, furniture, prams, cookers and cars. However much we deplore our waters becoming depositories for unwanted rubbish, such unsightly objects, so alien to the natural underwater environment, eventually become corroded. Their forms are softened by algal colonisation, and so they become important fish holding sites. Those pike more inclined to territorial habits will utilise these features as permanent holts, ousting smaller rivals and defending the site from any potential usurper. Pike will only be absent from such secure bases when they move off in search of prey.

Nomadic pike will roam using trenches, for these features are natural passageways as well as sites attractive to other species. Besides being patrol routes, trenches provide cover, and pike will select lies by the side of a trench at the conjunction of the base and the slope. In the case of territorial fish, such a lie may be permanent, while the more nomadic pike will favour a number of lies, dependent on where the last meal was obtained, water temperature, climatic variation and the location of prey shoals.

There are many variables, but if the angler is aware of and takes heed of such factors, he can at least make a reasonable deduction as to where some pike are likely to be encountered. Trenches leading to an area of deep water, frequented by prey as winter quarters, will certainly be used by pike moving in on the shoal to feed, as well as those who are replete and retiring to what might be termed 'digestive lies'. A very likely pike catching area will be where the mouth of the trench and the deep water coincide.

Other pike holding lies as well as patrol routes are the drop-offs to deeper water by islands. Islands are attractive to fish for, besides being free of bankside disturbance, they are natural landmarks for a shoal moving from one part of the water to another. A channel connecting two expanses of water has the effect of funnelling a shoal into a confined space as they pass through, and such narrows are a magnet for pike who can wait for their quarry, rather than having to expend energy hunting it. Of course pike will also move through such channels, and a strategically positioned bait is likely to be taken.

Promontories are another excellent interception point, whereby nomadic pike will be encountered. Such projections are landmarks used by predator and prey alike. The areas pike might be expected here are where the slope levels off, or even better in a trench, however insignificant, if one is situated somewhere just off the point. Without doubt this trench would be a well used fish highway for shoals rounding the promontory.

Unless some important underwater feature dictates otherwise, it is always more productive to fish off the windward side of a point. Even in calm conditions it is best to fish off the side of the promontory that last faced the wind. When fishing from the bank, the calm water on the lee side may look inviting but it hardly ever lives up to its promise.

Shallow bays or arms do not fish well in winter, but if there is a pronounced drop-off, or ledge off the mouth of the bay it should be considered a possible pike holding area. However, bays with a depth of ten feet or over that face the prevailing wind are always worth a try, particularly when the wind is strong.

Other more obvious pike holding locations need only a brief mention. For example, snags such as half or fully submerged trees, undercut banks and bankside vegetation are likely sites. Pike can often be found off any inflow of water however slight, usually lying in the deeper water beyond the silt edge. Water welling up from a spring or any other form of inflow is attractive to fish.

LARGE LAKES
Lakes seem to give off a feeling of timeless maturity, an atmosphere and intimacy that makes them seem easier to read than the featureless gravel pits and reservoirs. This gives the angler a great sense of confidence, but although large gravel pits have a reputation for being difficult to come to terms with, they are no harder than lakes. Possibly the reverse is nearer the truth.

There are shallow lakes with water of no greater depth than ten feet. Other lakes contain both shallows and deeps and there are some where all the water is over ten feet deep with no shallows to speak of at all. Normally the great majority of lowland lakes are shallower than reservoirs and the general run of gravel pits. With such a variety, it is only possible to consider one type of lake, those with variable depths between five and fifteen feet.

As a generalisation, the bottom contours will be far more even than in the gravel pits, gently shelving between shallows and deeps, and the lake bed will consist of layers of soft detritus overlaying clay, which is impervious to water seepage.

The prolific weed growth of summer will die off with winter's onset to form mats of rotting vegetation lying on the bottom. This relatively shallow water will cool rapidly, and unlike deep waters there will be little if any temperature variation in any part of the lake once winter conditions have stabilised. Equally, warm winds and the effect of sunlight can lead to a rise in temperatures. No doubt these factors account for the unpredictable feeding patterns of fish in shallow waters.

This knowledge is useful, for in lakes of this type pike can be expected to come on the feed after a sudden rise in air temperature, not immediately but the third day following the change would be the optimum time to try for them. Conversely a rapid drop in temperature will have the opposite effect, although once the cold conditions have stabilised some limited feeding will occur.

Because these waters are susceptible to climatic changes, the fish shoals do not act quite as predictably as those inhabiting deeper waters. There is no migration to permanent winter quarters, but as the water cools the smaller shoals that roam the water in summer join together in much larger, tighter concentrations. Except in severe weather these shoals will move slowly around the lake. This movement depends upon a host of variables such as wind direction, barometric pressure, food availability and air and water temperatures. In this way, fish will be very thin on the ground generally, while a few selected areas will be over-populated.

With a sudden drop in temperature these large shoals will move into the deepest water they can find, even though the temperature is the same as elsewhere. This can only be due to instinctive behaviour, inherent in the species, and once in the deeper water the shoal will ride close to the bottom while the cool conditions continue. With a marked increase in the temperature, often coinciding with warm oxygenating wind, the shoal will move towards the end of the lake facing the breeze and will be stationed higher in the water.

In some lakes roach prime throughout the year but in winter the fish show most often just after dawn, then again at dusk. However, in other waters visual location of the prey shoals cannot be relied upon. Here, useful information can be acquired for fish locations from match anglers or pleasure anglers on the water. Perhaps it is worth attending the odd match to note which sections of bank produce the best weight. These swims should be concentrated on, for with prey fish in the vicinity it is highly probable that some pike will be nearby.

Any of the fish location features that have been described may well be found in lakes, so do not need reiterating. However, with older more mature waters, sections of bank will be overgrown by a variety of marginal vegetation. One certain winter fish-holding swim can be found where the bank falls away almost vertically. The water will be relatively deep here, and overhung by brambles, scrub, or tree branches. Such a swim can harbour some of the best roach, and if perch are present in the water, their location here can be guaranteed. Similarly pike favour such a spot, lying on the bottom close to the vertical sides.

Steep-sided banks may conceal unexpected undercuts, caves that penetrate and are framed by a tangle of tree roots. Pike will occupy these holts both as ambush sites and for security. Deep overhung near bank swims, tend to be ignored by present day pike anglers, who seem to consider that distant casting is all-important. Of course these snag ridden swims are difficult, if not impossible to fish from the bank, but they can be tackled from a quietly positioned boat.

Some lake margins are colonised by reed beds. Reeds are beloved by pike who are prone to lie in, or alongside, the reed stems. If a lake contains reed-fringed islands, or islands formed by reeds alone, both may be considered good pike holding areas. An exciting method of fishing reed beds is to wind drift a float-suspended bait to within inches of the reed stems. This technique, developed by Broadland anglers, has proved extremely efficient.

All predatory fish are drawn to fry, and these tightly packed concentrations of tiny fish present an easily obtainable and nutritious food source that predators can exploit with the minimum expenditure of energy. In many lakes fry will concentrate in shallow water during the autumn and the shoals are easily identifiable. Occasionally a fry shoal can be pinpointed by the swirls and commotion made by attacking predators, a sight that has never ceased to thrill. However, more likely the shoal will betray its presence by the bright flashes of light reflected from tiny flanks as individual members twist and turn within the confines of the restless mass. It resembles an underwater microcosmic universe of twinkling stars. Later in November, those fry that have survived, by now little fish half the size of a minnow, will form more loosely knit formations in the surface layers of deeper water. These shoals are far more difficult to detect, but when the water is calm, often in the hour following the dawn, an observant spectator may notice that the mirrored surface may in defined areas appear to shiver. This phenomenon is due to the near invisible rises as myriads of tiny fish dimple the surface in unison.

Such small fish concentrations are a magnet for pike, but they rarely show at the surface, preferring to station themselves high in the water, so that when feeding they can cruise through the shoal, engulfing their prey by the mouthful. Pike that are preoccupied with such small food items are not so easy to tempt as it might appear. However, a small live or deadbait presented no more than three to five feet deep, or even at a pinch a tiny lure fished at the same depth, can be successful. A pike

that is caught when fry feeding is liable to disgorge its recent mouthfuls, unwittingly contributing to the supply of your bait. Such fortune should be exploited. These tiny unmarked fish may be mounted on a single hook, or two singles in tandem.

Circulation and wind currents

The three types of water under review are normally considered stillwaters, but this is a misnomer. Circulation and wind induced currents cause considerable water movement, whilst circulation is more pronounced in spring and autumn as the water alternatively warms up and cools down. Wind action can even cause currents to flow in opposite directions at the same time.

As water cools in autumn the surface layers tend to sink and are replaced by warmer water rising upwards. In this way circulation through the water occurs. Once all the water has cooled down to four degrees centigrade, at which temperature water is at its heaviest, circulation ceases, for when the surface water cools down further it no longer sinks but remains as a cold layer above the heavier water. The deep water remains throughout the winter at a constant four degrees. Consequently the water near to the bottom is the warmest, and this is the reason why fish migrate to the deeps during the colder months.

However, in exceptional climatic conditions this stability may be affected due to the wind induced currents. Prolonged periods of strong wind push the surface layer in the same direction as the wind is blowing, thus forming a current which piles up against the windward bank. This water then forms a counter current flowing in the opposite direction, rather akin to waves rebounding from sea walls and moving out to sea again. If this wind is cold, the opposite current will remain above the warmer water, but if the wind is warm and blows for long enough it can warm the surface layer to the same temperature as the deeper water. As the surface layer now sinks, a little circulation occurs which ceases when all the water reaches four degrees. If, and such conditions are rare, this surface layer becomes slightly warmer than the water beneath it, it remains at the surface. It may even extend beneath the surface while the wind still blows.

Fish react to temperature changes, so when such conditions prevail, they move into this slightly warmer and well-oxygenated water. In fact, when all the water remains at its temperature of four degrees centigrade, which at best may only last for a few hours, the bottom is no warmer than anywhere else. So, the shoal fish could be stationed at any depth. This may well account for those days when weather conditions appear ideal but when baits presented on or near the bottom are not effective. But with shoals of prey fish moving higher in the water, the feeding pike must enter the same depth band if it is to locate its prey. Therefore a bait fished at this optimum depth is far more likely to be encountered by a pike and taken.

When fixed bungs and pilot floats were standard piking gear, nobody ever seemed to fish bait any deeper than four to five feet, whatever the depth of water. I used the same method both before and just after the war. We all caught pike and provided the water was free from ice, weather conditions worried us not at all. I actually caught a twenty-six pound fish on a small roach presented three feet under the surface in water over twelve feet deep. What is food for thought is that a series of sharp frosts had caused ice to form at the lake edge, and some of the water was becoming covered in cat ice. Now, whatever the conditions, I always fish one bait high in the water, and do not rely entirely on deep fished baits. I

suspect that I have over the years missed catching many a good pike through being too hidebound and conservative in my methods.

Recording features

This section will deal with how to survey the underwater terrain using both a boat and an echo sounder. A power boat is essential, not as some may think to speed up the work, for by steaming around at a rate of knots a great deal of vital information will be missed, even when using the most up to date echo sounder or graph recorder. Power is most useful when moving upwind as anyone who has had to row a long distance into the teeth of a strong breeze knows only too well. The only feasible way to map big waters is to employ an echo sounder, or even better a graph recorder. The first may set you back up to one hundred pounds, and the second even five hundred pounds. Perhaps you may consider it pretty pointless mentioning equipment which is beyond the means of all except the most affluent, but like anglers in the USA who set so much store by graph recorders, I predict that in the next few years both angling clubs and smaller groups sharing in the cost will ensure their increasing use.

The old 'steam' method of ascertaining the depths by lead line is far too tedious and time consuming when tackling large expanses of water. Besides, the method is also very limited in scope, for while depth variations could be obtained with reasonable accuracy, the majority of fish holding features are bound to be missed. However, a sounding line is extremely useful in one respect, so mine remains in good order. The heavy cone shaped sea lead has a wide diameter hole bored into the flat base. This is packed with Vaseline or line grease, which is also smeared over the whole of the lead itself. This is known in naval parlance

Above *Tony Lovell begins his Arctic pike saga with a maelstrom of flying spray and ice chips. The temperature is well below freezing and the ice crust is ten inches thick.*

Below *A bait is lowered into the hole and the rod set up on an optonic and tripod rod rest.*

*A pike is hooked and the fight beneath
the ice begins. Tony Lovell kneels to
get a better grip and to stop himself
being spun by the running fish.*

Above *The pike surfaces.*

Below *The fish, finally beaten, waits to be lifted clear.*

*Tony holds the sleek mid-double clear
of the ice for a second, before sliding it
back into its dark winter home.*

as 'arming the lead'. It enables samples of the bottom composition to be brought inboard for examination as mud, sand and gravel adhere to the grease layer. Modern electronic equipment can indicate whether the nature of the bottom is hard or soft and even the depth of soft deposits are recorded, but the actual consistency can only be guessed at.

Echo sounders have been available for some years, but now the more efficient graph recorders can be obtained. Possibly the best for fish finding surveillance is the Lowrance Eagle Mach I. It is not the most expensive in the Lowrance range, but it does provide all the information that the pike angler could ever wish for. This model has twenty-four depth ranges from nought to ten feet, and nought to one thousand feet! There is an expansion feature that magnifies the size of the bottom echoes. Not only can the smallest bottom irregularity be charted, but the locality of shoaling fish can be precisely recorded, as can larger individual fish.

The ethics of using such equipment will certainly be the subject of hot debate. In the past, successful anglers have had to develop a keen sense of watercraft, which allied to experience and not a little intuitive guesswork helped them locate fish with some degree of expertise. The main objective in going fishing is, I presume, to catch fish, so the more efficiently the quarry can be located, the better the chances. Certainly anglers of little experience will be able to compete on more equal terms with those who have painstakingly acquired a lifetime of knowledge. However, even when the quarry has been found, the experienced, thinking angler will still be able to exploit the situation far more successfully than the beginner. The march of progress cannot be halted and the next generation of anglers will make use of fish finding devices without a qualm. The following passage is designed to help in charting an unknown water by echo sounder or graph recorder.

The first step is to acquire a map showing the water and its perimeter in some detail. The Ordnance Survey 1:25,000 first or second series normally covers six and a quarter square miles at a scale of two and a half inches to a mile. This second series is best, for the first series are derived from pre-1939 surveys and many large gravel pits had yet to be excavated then. The process of replacing the first with the second series is still going on, so it is possible that the latter will still be unavailable. In this case it is worth a letter to the Ordnance Survey Information Department, Romsey Road, Maybush, Southampton SO9 4DH. Even if a map is yet to be published, aerial surveys will be undertaken and a photograph or scale drawing of an as yet unmapped water will be available.

Having obtained a map, make an enlarged drawing of the water's perimeter on a piece of white card, of such a size that it can easily be stowed amongst your tackle. The card can be glued to a piece of hardboard and protected by a plastic folder. At the same time, make a larger drawing on to which important features can be recorded; naturally this master chart remains at home. Complete accuracy is not strictly necessary as the chart is not to be used for navigation, but for those who would like to be a little more meticulous it can be achieved quite simply. Place a transparent sheet, tracing paper is suitable, over the map of the water and carefully record the perimeter outline. This tracing can then be projected on to a vertical surface by an overhead projector to the required size. Most schools, colleges and offices have such equipment and to create an enlargement is only a few minutes' work.

The next stage is to transfer from the map to both charts important features, both in the water such as islands, valve towers and jetties, and those on the surrounding land such as buildings, telegraph poles, pylons, small clumps of trees, and eventually other prominent landmarks which will be noticed when afloat.

This section is not about to turn into a treatise on navigation and pilotage, but the ability to take a compass bearing of an object, which anyone is perfectly capable of, is immensely useful for re-locating underwater features quickly. When afloat, a stout hard-covered notebook is essential for writing down an exact description of each feature as it is discovered. In the notebook should go two compass bearings that intersect at that position.

To get these compass bearings, an inexpensive hand bearing compass can be obtained from any chandler that supplies the yachting fraternity. These compasses point to magnetic North which varies annually from true North and much will be made of this in the instructional leaflet. This variation is of no consequence in relation to the simple charting procedures that need to be undertaken, so it can be ignored. However, do remember that magnetic compasses will give a false reading when used in the proximity of a metal object, so don't lean on the outboard, or sit even near by, particularly when the engine is running. Even a pair of unhooking forceps hanging from a lapel could cause a magnetic compass to deviate by a couple of degrees.

Half a day spent running up, down and across the water with the sounder or recorder operating will indicate not only the depth variations in general, but give some idea of the size and extent of fish shoals. Then, a more thorough survey selected from this information can be made. If the wind is suitable, a slow drift is ideal. If it is not, get out the oars, unless the outboard can be throttled right down without oiling the plug. The more slowly the ground is covered the better, otherwise many bottom features will be missed.

Whenever an important feature shows on the display, note the depth, take two bearings and record the feature type. Number the entry in the notebook. Remember the angle between objects from which bearings are taken should not be greater than 135° or less than 45°. A 90° angle will give the most accurate 'fix'. At the end of the day results can be roughly marked on the chart, and recorded in the notebook. A typical entry might be

No 32. Broken ground. Boulders? Approximately 10 yds by 15 yds in area. Depth over feature 18 ft. Valve tower 047. White house 132.

These compass bearings are all that is required to locate the area of the boulder strewn bottom whenever it is necessary. In order to do so, position the boat on one line of bearing. For example position the boat so that the valve tower bears 047, then check the bearing of the white house. If the bearing is less than 132, steer towards the valve tower, which should of course continue to bear 047, until the white house bears 132. The boat will then be over the broken ground. Alternatively, if the bearing of the white house is more than 132, steer away from the valve tower on the opposite course to the line of bearing which is 047 plus 180, a course of 227.

As it is unlikely the boat will be fitted with a fixed navigational compass, the bearing of the valve tower must be checked at intervals until the white house is on the correct bearing of 132. Because of the effect of wind and surface current, and the possibly that the original compass bearings were perhaps not quite accurate by a degree or so, it might be necessary to circle the immediate area using the recorder until the feature appears on the display once more.

Obviously, even with the aid of electronic gadgetry, it takes time to survey a large water. It is perhaps more sensible to

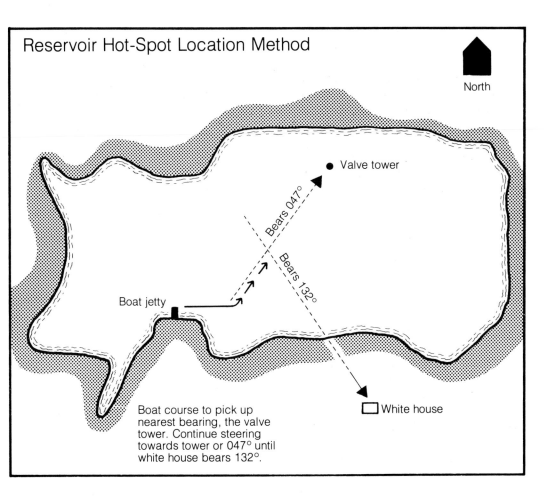

Reservoir Hot-Spot Location Method

North

Valve tower

Bears 047°

Bears 132°

Boat jetty

Boat course to pick up
nearest bearing, the valve
tower. Continue steering
towards tower or 047° until
white house bears 132°.

White house

thoroughly chart one portion first, and
when a number of potential pike holding
areas have been discovered they can be
fished. Later on further sections can be
surveyed likewise, until eventually the
whole water has been covered.

The big fish enigma

I shall end this chapter with an enigma,
with an inexplicable mystery over which I
can only theorise. I have often been approached when fishing, as no doubt all of
us have been, and been regaled with stories
concerning a monster pike which is re-
puted to live in the water. Many stillwaters, large or small and even ponds, are

subject to such legends. Tales like this are
the stuff of fishing. Though great fun to
listen to, and enjoyable as they are, I used
always to discount them. Not any more!

There have been waters with no particular reputation for producing large pike, as
well as those which have been hard fished
for just a few good ones each season, where
the rotting carcass of a huge pike has been
discovered. These are fish far larger than
any ever caught, or even suspected of
being in the water. What is strange is that
while alive, these great pikes never took
any of the bait alive or dead that they must
have encountered from time to time.

I know of one large lake where an angler
was quietly fishing for bream from a boat.

His keep net, containing a number of fish around the five pound mark, was hanging over the side. Quite suddenly the boat slewed round, jerked against some mooring weights, whilst the net was pulled out horizontally. The tail of the net was being shaken from side to side in a smother of spray. When the commotion subsided, the angler rowed back to the boathouse, saying that an enormous pike, which he had clearly seen, was the culprit. This event was so traumatic, so frightening that the chap said that nothing on earth would persuade him to venture out on to the water again.

Perhaps you think this is a tall story, but there is more to come. Bill Giles who is not given to exaggeration, tells of an angler who was fishing in the same area of this lake the following year. He had hooked a bream, estimated to weigh about six pounds, which was played out and lying on its side ready for netting. Then as suddenly as before, a huge form, a crocodile of a fish, materialised, grabbed the bream and then took it down deep leaving a great swirling vortex on the surface. Not unnaturally the light line departed and the great fish was seen no more.

Whenever time could be spared, I concentrated on that part of the lake where the pike had been seen, using hefty herrings and even larger mackerel, not to mention livebaits twice the size of those I normally prefer to use. After two consecutive seasons fishing with little to show for all the effort, except for the odd second of tremulous excitement whenever a float slid below the surface, I admitted defeat. Provided that pike was alive and still frequenting the area I was fishing, why did it ignore three-quarters of a pound of fresh, nutritious mackerel? One reason could have been that a pike liking only to feed on large fish would require very few to satisfy its needs. Therefore, on the odd times when I was fishing, I could have coincided with digestive periods and consequent inactivity. But

what seems far more likely is that the pike fed selectively on one species only – bream and large ones at that. Bream are abundant in the lake, averaging five pounds in weight, and they would of course have been available to that pike throughout the year. Perhaps if I had used a large bream as bait I might have fared better, but when that possibility did eventually occupy my thoughts, the owner prohibited the use of boats in that very area of the lake.

Now, I come to the theory which I think might explain the enigma, the mystery as to why, just occasionally an extra large pike is discovered that has died from old age, even in those waters that are fished by experienced pike anglers. No doubt a few pike, perhaps due to some genetic peculiarity, grow larger and more quickly than others of the same year class. Amongst these fish there is possibly just the occasional one, that once it has reached a certain size, chooses to feed on one species only. Possibly a good example is Clive Loveland's Knipton Reservoir pike. This thirty-nine pound fish was taken on a sizeable four pound jack pike. Perhaps it fed exclusively on its own species, for it must have seen a whole variety of more normal baits in Knipton which attracted plenty of pike anglers, at least in those days.

It seems to be quite feasible that a few of those tales of monster pike may well contain some truth. For if fish exist that only feed on pike, large bream, big trout or sizeable tench they are unlikely to be caught on the more normal run of baits. Therefore, their presence remains unsuspected, that is until one shows itself, like that bream-eating pike. So are the pikeman's legends born.

Who in his right mind, even if he could

Opposite *This 31lb 10oz pike is treated with great care by John Watson, held over an expanse of wetted sacking and canvas.*

devise a suitable hook rig, could fish day after day with monstrous baits such as five pound pike and five pound bream, just on the off chance of catching one huge, near mythical fish that might, only might, lurk in that particular water? Whether such fish exist is arguable, but to misquote slightly, 'There are more things in heaven and earth than are dreamt of in our philosophies'. And so, when I am quietly fishing I often ponder on such things.

JACK LIVEBAITS

by Paul Snepp

Chris Turnbull 85

Further to this 'big fish enigma', we have received a contribution from Paul Snepp. We both are convinced of the correctness of what Paul has to say.

The use of large livebait has always been a matter of great controversy. To use another man's specimen fish as bait is both contemptuous and unethical. Yet, as some of the photographs and text in Fred Buller's books so graphically prove, fish, pike, have the ability to consume prey that are up to and over thirty per cent of their own weight. There is scientific evidence to suggest that as pike grow bigger the prey they select gets larger.

I believe that most creatures have a fundamental ability to learn, discern, and take action based on previous experience. I apply this to the pike, which is funda-

mentally a predator, and deduce that for the majority of the time in the majority of environments the successful predator, the bigger pike, is selective in its type of food. The first choice of these bigger pike is to consume any dead or dying food item that they happen across. Their second choice is to take the largest, single, live food item that they can catch, balanced against the effort they will need to expend catching that item. We know how successful dead-baits are. Large livebaits are equally so. In waters that contain large stocks of jack pike, I am convinced that they fill a vital role, and are actively sought out by large pike.

My suggestion is that, where viable, you do use large livebaits, and that you restrict your choice of bait solely to jack pike. These, I believe to be the most efficient, and they are neither lost to fellow anglers nor to the water from where they came.

Over the course of several years and in diverse waters, I have been a party to the development of the technique that works very efficiently in both presentation and satisfactory hooking when using jack livebaits up to two pounds in weight. Firstly, I go 'over the top' with tackle strength. Rods should be long, through action, between three and four pounds test curve. Lines should never be under fifteen pounds breaking strain and must float. I never undertake this method of fishing without at least two hundred metres of line on the spool, unless I am in or have available a boat in which to remain in close contact to the taking fish.

The terminal rig is a standard paternoster beefed up. The float should be as streamlined as possible, yet capable of withstanding the surges of baits of this size. The lead will need to be a minimum of two ounces. A trace of three size eight treble hooks has proved ideal. One hook goes into the root of one pectoral fin, one into the root of the anal fin, and the other just forward of the dorsal fin.

With the exception of very deep waters, the bait should be presented at, or just above, mid-water and in very deep water it should be held at least ten feet away from the bottom. The bait should be placed well away from any sub-surface cover in a totally exposed position. This causes the bait to remain very active, as if aware of its peril, sending out those attractive vibrations throughout the water and remaining highly visible. It is tethered and unable to run for cover.

If you can place a bait from a boat then row away from it, fine. If you are confined to the bank, do not concern yourself in fruitless attempts to cast a bait any great distance. Just lob it out into clear water. It is this point that convinces me that these jacks are selected. For often the spot they

are taken in is far away from the areas one needs to cast more conventional baits into to secure a run. Further, on days when we have been able to offer a selection of baits fished in a variety of ways close to the jack rig, the only runs have come to the jack. This has now occurred on far too many occasions to be dismissed as chance, coincidence, or whatever. No! These jacks have been selected.

Presumably because a large prey fish puts up a fair resistance to the pike you will not find that the fish is put off by the large lead or float. Dropped runs are a very rare occurrence, and have usually been because of the pike swimming into or through some sub-surface snag.

What follows is inviolate, and as foolproof as any method can be. When the run occurs, immediately pick up the rod and control line spill. The pike will begin swimming away with the bait. Broadly speaking, the larger the water the further it will swim. Sometimes it will move for a very great distance, perhaps in circles, or up and down a contour line, often for some considerable time. Concentrate, remain in as close contact as possible. Eventually the pike will stop, often the float disappears, or violently bobs up and down. At this point, and not before, wind down hard and pull into the pike as normal. This striking pattern has been perfected at the expense of losing many catches for fear of deep hooking. Following this method, I have not seen one badly hooked pike, which I feel sure is foremost in all our minds.

There is no ultimate bait, but it is yet another successful method to add to our repertoire. It is a method that has, to my certain knowledge, produced twenty pound pike from a water where none has been caught before, and it is responsible on several waters for producing the heaviest fish to date.

What Dennis, Tony and Paul have had to

say about bait is not a gimmick. Bait variation is as important in pike fishing as it is in carp fishing, but until now this has been realised by only a few pikers in the past.

That pike do learn rapidly was experienced by J.B. in December 1984, tackling a small two acre pit which none the less had good fish in it. He used conventional baits throughout. No fish that he caught were well hooked, and several came adrift despite being given a perilously long time to turn the quite ordinary, sea fish deadbaits. Even more strange was the number of times the totally quiet water surface would be disturbed by pike, rolling or splashing in the immediate vicinity of the float. After a few days, this unusual habit became very frequent, but although J.B. would see pike right over his baits in this way, only once did a run develop. On many occasions, the bait was left untouched.

It seems likely that these large fish had become wary of conventional baits over the years and, although still attracted by the smell of the juices, were alarmed by the actual sight of the offerings. When Roger Miller began to fish the pit with a live trout, a bait which none of the fish had been caught on before, he was at once rewarded with a twenty-one pounder, which took very positively indeed. Further experiments were planned, but cut short by the ferocious weather in early 1985.

Norfolk Broadlands

This was once the centre of massive peat excavations, but now its major industry, which is both highly commercial and environmentally devastating, is the holiday and boating trade. The summer season extends increasingly into the winter months, restricting serious angling throughout this large area of broads and rivers. By the end of October, however, the motor cruiser traffic abates enough, in parts of the Broadlands, for the pike angler to contemplate sport, and as winter progresses it is still possible to be lost on several remote reed-surrounded broads and to savour the essence of Broadland piking. The peace will be broken only by the lonely boom of a bittern, or the sound of the Norfolk reed-cutter gathering his living as did his fathers for generations before him.

So much a loner by nature, a hunter and trapper, the dedicated pike angler has everything at his fingertips on the Broads. He has both large open and small shallow waters. He has shallow, narrow rivers such as the Thurne. He can fish larger, slower moving rivers such as the Bure. Or he can choose the Waveney and Yare, which are often described as men's waters – deep, heavily tidal and fast moving. If ever there were a pike angler's paradise, then surely the Broadlands, famous for large pike and home of both the old and the new English records, is the place.

The pike of the Broads are not only famous for their size, but also their shape.

These are long beasts with huge 'bream-shovelling' heads, in complete contrast to the short, thick-shouldered and deep fish of trout lakes and reservoirs. The Broads fish are lazy too, for they have abundant supplies of fodder fish throughout their environment and need not work hard to obtain nourishment, and of course weight. Perhaps this laziness is part of the reason for their immediate liking for deadbaits.

The Broadland area does of course comprise waters other than the Broads and their parent rivers. There are large numbers of lakes and gravel pits all capable of supporting large pike, and even trout, waters such as that from which J.B. caught his magnificent thirty-six pound fish. However, the methods for tackling these in no way differ from similar waters in other parts of the country which we have covered in other sections of the book. So, here we concentrate entirely on the true Broadlands.

There are four major waterway systems of interest to the Broadland pike angler – the rivers Bure, Thurne, Waveney and Yare. Of these four the Thurne and Bure with their associated broads are the most famous, and the broads of the Yare and Waveney receive relatively little attention from pike anglers at present. The actual River Yare is almost totally neglected and although the River Waveney is fished in parts of its lower reaches, there is still scope for much research. These two rivers, however, are not typical of the Norfolk Broads and for any angler considering their challenge, then the river section of this book will be of more use to them.

There is, however, one 'broad' on the Waveney system which could well be capable of a truly enormous pike and that is Fritton Lake. Here again, although this is almost certainly a broad, even as its name suggests, its characteristics conform largely with any other big open lake. For this reason it is sufficient to note its existence and inviting potential but the approach to such water would be found more in the chapter by Vic Bellars than in this Broadland section.

We turn then to the true Broadland rivers of the Bure and Thurne and their numerous connected broads. Immediately we notice a difference in character of the two systems. Furthermore it soon becomes obvious that each and every broad has its own personality and idiosyncrasies. On the Bure system the labours of the turf-diggers some 700 or more years ago, left us with waters on an average of twelve to sixteen feet in depth. Now, however, the silting and encroachment has affected each broad in its own way, and so created a series of waters of individual character, each demanding its own approach. Compare, for example, the deeper Decoy Broad and its adjacent shallow neighbours, the Hoveton Little and Great Broads.

Some of the Bure broads have a salt tide influence, like the South Walsham Broad. Then too, there are the large fresh water reserves, the Ormesby system, unpolluted by the motor cruisers, retaining some of their original depth, and possibly one of the most typical examples of a perfectly balanced water with a pyramid pike population and all fish at present at their peak.

Moving on to the much shorter, shallower River Thurne and its broads we find a system which provides true shallow water pike fishing, in an environment that screams pike from one reedy bay to the next. Of course it has a tragic history. In August and September 1969, prymnesium struck at the last great pike boom that had seen the capture of Peter Hancock's forty pound giant. Prymnesium isn't really a disease at all, but a poisoning of the fish caused by a microscopic plant or algae.

The algae lives in salt and brackish water, and under favourable conditions multiplies rapidly to produce an algae bloom. Chemicals released by the mass of algae poison all types of fish in the area. We stress that the poison is released by the living algae, and not, as is commonly thought, when the algae dies.

Prymnesium toxin exerts its lethal effect on all gill breathing animals. It works by making the gills permeable to a wide range of toxic substances such as copper which normally cannot enter the fish. The toxin also kills by causing the fish's cells, especially the red blood cells, to disintegrate. The effectiveness of the toxin varies with water conditions, being greatest in fresh water. It is easy to see how the algae could multiply during brackish water conditions in the Norfolk Broads, producing a toxin which would be carried with the tides up the rivers Bure, Thurne and Ant, poisoning the fish in its path.

As with so many great natural tragedies, the Thurne and its broads have an almost unbelievable record of recovery. Nostalgia surrounds the Thurne broads, and those magnificent fish of the days of Pye and Hancock, constantly come to mind whilst spending a day there on the system. The wonder is, though, that our children will sit there in years to come, remembering the 1980s, and the fish the system is now producing.

Why the Thurne system produces fish which, on average, are several pounds larger than their Bure system relatives, is cause for speculation. Perhaps it is the heavier salt influence which has some effect on the environment. Perhaps the salt in-

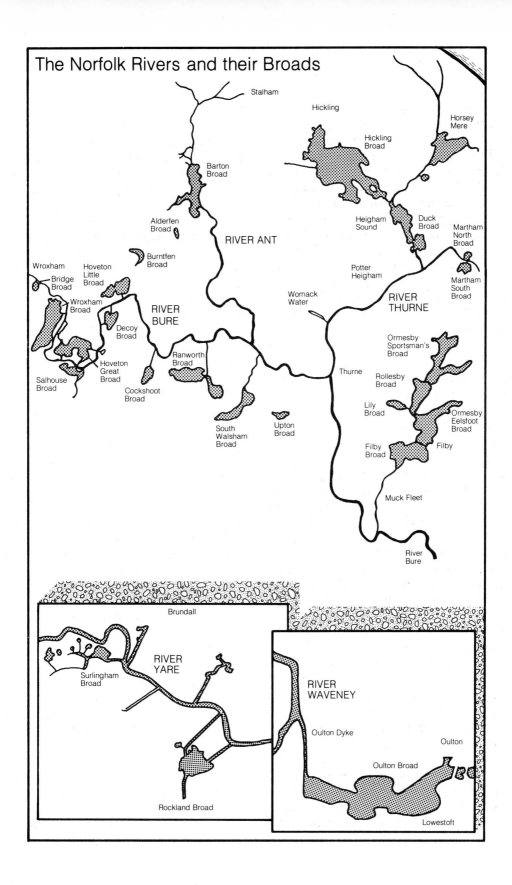

The Norfolk Rivers and their Broads

fluence helps luscious weed growth which results in a vibrant food cycle. Or perhaps in some way the salt helps the fish to live longer, for it certainly seems, on the limited research conducted, that these fish do enjoy longer lives.

In all probability it is a combination of the factors, and although the salt probably is part of the answer – the Horsey water actually tastes of salt – it is also likely that the soil structure and the original purpose for which these broads were excavated is of importance. Indeed these broads were not excavated to the same depths as their Bure counterparts. The excavations ceased at some six feet and present opinion suggests that they were not even excavated primarily for their peat, unlike the Bure broads, but that it was the clay which was needed for building materials.

So we have stretches of broads, scattered over with windmills, flatlands, with hundreds upon hundreds of acres containing large pike, largely unfished and with only a few popular venues attracting attention. These are the waters currently at the centre of the country's, if not the world's, attention. They are now at a peak, but yet every rise precedes a fall so what might be their future?

Certainly, for the next few years, unless prymnesium strikes again, or the sea once more breaches its barriers, the prospects for the Broadland angler throughout the Norfolk Broads, are very good indeed. In the Pike Anglers' Club Magazine, *Pikelines*, in 1982 M.P. referred to the big pike cycle and his belief that the Norfolk Broads were about to experience such a cycle. He predicted then, that we were on the eve of a new English pike record, and that it would fall firstly to a Broadland pike but ultimately perhaps to big reservoir fish. As we set pen to paper tonight, in February 1985, we write with some satisfaction having just congratulated Neville Fickling on his magnificent forty-one pound six ounce English record pike. So the first part of a prediction has come true. Neville's fish was returned in perfect condition to the water so there is unquestionably a chance of recapturing the same fish, and the record falling once more. Also of course we can now speculate as to whether there are further fish of perhaps even greater weight to be caught during this present cycle. We are eternal optimists, and consider this to be probable or, at least, that the Norfolk Broads will, during the next few years, produce one or two more fish over forty pounds. There is a great deal of water, and even if a few waters of the area become over-fished, there is still an excess of virgin territory for the thinking angler to explore and conquer.

Opposite *Dave Plummer shows how to weigh a 30lb pike. The strong canvas sling stops the pike falling and being injured.*

BROADLAND PIKING

by Steve Harper

The old-fashioned idea of a Broadland angler is of a lone fisherman, in a boat on a reed fringed broad with gaff, bung and live-bait. Unfortunately for the pike, a few of these characters still exist, but now they are thankfully few and far between compared with only a few years ago. This is probably the direct result of an enlightened approach to the pike and pike angling. I believe it is the reward for much hard work done by the Pike Anglers' Club of Great Britain.

Pike angling is constantly changing and no more so than in the Broadlands. Norfolk, the county that is the country's undisputed pike 'Mecca', harbours a hard core of some of England's top pike anglers. And with many other experienced pike men travelling from far and wide to sample the Broadlands' treasures, it is not surprising that many of the latest developments in pike angling tackle, techniques and thinking have been developed in, or stem directly from, Norfolk.

And so, the average Broadland piker is more likely nowadays to be equipped with carbon rods, multiplier reels, barbless trebles and all the other accessories that go to make a pike angler in the 1980s.

Boats

To fish these large expanses of open water and the miles of tidal rivers, a boat is absolutely essential. There are the odd bank fishing spots that regularly produce large pike, but there is no point cutting chances to the bare minimum. So, the answer is to get organised with a sturdy reliable boat and engine. It is always preferable to fish from your own boat. At least then you know that the anchor cables will reach bottom in six feet of water, that the rowlocks will not fall out at the slightest provocation and that you will not have to remove half the broad before you can start fishing!

One quite well-known pike angler, who had not been boat fishing before, was heard to remark on his first visit to Broadland 'Can you stand up in these things?' Well, once you have learned the basics, and feel confident afloat, there is certainly no need to be overcautious. It is best always to stand when striking, for instance, and I defy anyone to answer the call of nature when sitting down in full winter pike kit!

Once you own a boat, the next step is to customise it with pike fishing in mind. The first essential is wall to wall underlay for the deck. Soft rubber matting or carpet will do, but whatever it is, it needs to completely cover the bottom of the boat and preferably to cover up the sides as well. This not only protects the pike, which is its main function, but also reduces noise and helps to keep your feet warm! Long anchor ropes with pulleys and cleats, clip-on rod rests and many other ideas are all optional extras that help to make life that much easier and the day that much more enjoyable.

One trick that was used by the old school

Roger Miller has just landed John
Bailey's first 20lb pike.

of Norfolk pike fishermen and seems to
have been almost forgotten, is to tie up to
the reeds when fishing the rivers or the
fringes of a broad, using short, extra
lengths of light rope, tied to bow and stern.
It is the most stable way I know of securing
a boat, and there is no risk of a fish fouling
the anchor line or pole.

Once you are afloat, it is impossible to be
too quiet. We know how many fish we
catch. I wonder how many we scare away?
It is surprising how some very cautious and
quiet bank anglers can suddenly transform
into noisy, clumsy novices the minute they
set foot in a boat.

Tackle

Boat fishing is extremely tough on tackle.
Rods especially take a real battering. Rings
and line must be checked regularly if break-
ages are to be avoided.

In America, there is a vogue for shorter
rods for boat fishing and I have heard this
opinion voiced in this country also. It is a
view I find hard to accept. Twelve feet is my
ideal length for a pike rod, whether it be for
bank or boat fishing. There are often those
occasions in a boat when the longer rod is
appreciated. Turning a fish from the
anchor cable is only one example.

As for reels, if you have not used a
multiplier from a boat, then you don't
know what you are missing. Only when
you have taken your gloves off a dozen
times to replace the line in the elastic band
after the winds have rocked the boat, or
when the run music sounds as a take pulls

line against a loosened ratchet, can you really appreciate a multiplier to the full. I have used multipliers now since 1972 and have found only one problem that should be watched out for. If you cast and forget to pull in the spool release button, and get or have a take on the retrieve, it is impossible to push in the button to give line once it is under pressure. The only course of action is to pull back on the line (and the fish!) thereby slackening off pressure on the spool, and then quickly pushing in the button. If you are not careful, this can result in one of two things. Either the pike is alarmed and rejects the bait after feeling pressure, or the spool suddenly jumps to life and the fish takes line rapidly inducing a severe bird's nest attack. Either way you lose, so be warned! Apart from that one drawback, which rarely happens, multipliers are the ultimate for Broadland pike fishing.

Location

As for locating pike on the Broads, well, that can sometimes be no easy matter. However, there are one or two dodges that can be used to good effect.

The first is to move swims regularly. Now this may sound basic, but it is surprising how long we will give a swim if 'it produced last week' or 'it always fishes when the weather is like this' and so on. To be quite honest with you, pike are usually pretty stupid and if you have a feeding fish in the swim, the chances are, if you are using live-baits and deadbaits, you will have a take within twenty minutes. Forty-five minutes maximum, with no sign of a fish, and it is time for a move. Of course, there are exceptions to this rule. If you have a hot-spot that is on, then up to two hours may be spent there. But, it is no good sitting on a hot swim all day if at the end of it you have not had a take!

It is an idea to plan the day out. Try to allocate time to swims that you know will produce at certain times of the day. By all means, start at the favourite swim and perhaps finish the day there also, but be sure that you have searched out as much of the water as possible if things are slow. If a fish has taken, start the clock running again, but do not hang around longer than another hour after a take if nothing else is forthcoming. After all, you might just be on the very edge of a hot-spot, and that move could mean the difference between an average day and a red letter one.

As fishing time is precious, it also pays to make the most of each forty-five minutes in a new swim. Do not just anchor, cast out and hope the baits will do the work for you. Work them constantly. Twitch livebaits regularly to keep them on the move or better still, pull them back a foot or two, to keep them lively. Deadbaits can also be twitched and moved, and if nothing has happened within twenty minutes or so, swap a livebait with a deadbait, or a smelt with a herring, and so on.

Moving swims regularly can also be incorporated with searching out a section of water using a grid or straight line system, and dropping down further than casting distance at each move. It is impossible to search out a complete broad thoroughly in one day, so concentrate on one area and if it does not produce then try another area on your next visit. It is surprising how soon a picture begins to take shape.

The Broads are by nature very uniform in depth, and this is in itself a hindrance to location. So, if a drastic change in depth is found, then it is always worth fishing there. This also applies to all features that stand out from the usual. These include bays, points, overhanging trees, dyke entrances, adjoining river mouths and several other

Opposite *Martyn Page afloat on the Ormesby system, equipped with multipliers.*

such features. Anywhere that a pike might ambush its prey is where you might ambush the pike! There are other obvious pointers, such as fry showing, diving birds catching fry and other anglers being successful. So keep your eyes open to all that happens around you.

On the tidal rivers, location seems easier than on the Broads and this can sometimes be the case. But, pike do have a nasty habit of moving up and down rivers chasing their prey and may be literally miles from where they were the week before. A river does somehow seem easier to come to grips with. When you eye the vast expanse of Hickling or Heigham sounds for the first time it can be awe-inspiring. Even the widest Norfolk river can be cast across, and to fish a stretch systematically, dropping down regularly seems an obvious way to go about fishing. This has been much more successful than random swim selection.

To take the moving theme a stage further, float trolling live or deadbaits is a sure way of covering more pike and hopefully inducing more takes. This method can be used on the Broads, but it is more suited to slow tidal rivers such as the Bure. It can be used purely to locate concentrations of pike, or as a fish catching method in its own right. It is a real eye opener when you first discover the potential of float trolling. Swims that have seemed dead to static forms of live and deadbaiting suddenly spring to life when trolled through.

Float trolling does have many drawbacks. On large open broads the wind is the main problem. It is impossible to keep a slow, straight course in even a moderate wind. Weed, strong flows, boats and other anglers are all potential problems for the would-be troller. But if you can troll efficiently it is inevitable that you will cover more pike and receive more takes.

Live and deadbaits

Deadbaits are renowned for their big fish catching abilities, but livebaits are still the most effective way of catching numbers of fish. It may be that if a big fish is to come out, it will be on a deadbait, but livebaits enable you to build up a better overall picture of a water's pike population. It is sometimes said that the water is a 'deadbait water', or that a water is a 'livebait water'. I cannot think, however, of one Norfolk water where I would only take lives or deads if I had the choice of both.

The deadbait rig I use is largely standard, but is very versatile in different conditions of light and flow. The hooking arrangement is the usual barbless two treble rig with different numbers of swan shot or sliding leads depending on the size of bait. The point to remember when deadbaiting from a boat is always to use a float. I have seen on occasion people free-lining and legering deadbaits from boats. This is just asking for deep hooked pike.

The floats I use are home-made self cockers. They are long and thin, up to twelve inches, and are painted either half white and half red, or half black and half red. They have a small eye at each end, which means they can be reversed for differing light conditions by using a clip link sliding on the main line. The swan shots on this link can also be adjusted for flow or drift to keep the float in plain view.

As for the actual deadbaits themselves, all the usual baits still work well on Broadland, although it is the slightly more unusual baits like smelts or eel sections that are producing more and more as fishing pressure increases. I have recently been experimenting with cocktail deadbaits. This really stemmed from not knowing what to do with the small smelts that are always left at the end of a batch. So I decided to hook them on to a herring or mackerel. This trick seems to have worked, but whether it

The junction of Candle Dyke and the River Thurne has seen the capture of many big fish. This angler is rowing up the Dyke towards Heigham Sounds and Hickling Broad.

is, in spite, rather than, because of, I still am not sure. Another variation on the same theme, and one that I have more confidence in, is the use of a small livebait, lip hooked to a deadbait trace. The combination of a live and deadbait is mouth watering. Pike can hardly resist it!

Where livebaiting is concerned one basic rig is employed, which at very short notice can be changed for use as paternoster, free roving or trolling. The last two are in fact the same rig, the only difference being that for trolling the bait is mounted pointing up the trace and is usually of smaller size. Extra shot are also added to keep the bait well down.

I still favour the very small streamlined floats for livebaiting. There is a vogue at the moment for ping-pong ball type pike floats. These may not offer as much resistance to a taking pike as the old bung, but they must certainly tire a bait quicker and impede its free movement. It is advisable in my opinion to use the smallest float that will do the job.

For paternostering, I usually use a sunken float, ensuring a very tight line at all times. It seems logical that if you can see the float, then the rig is not fishing as tightly as it should. Slack line means incorrectly fished baits and usually tangles. It is nice to watch a float all day, but if it will catch more fish, I will fish a sunken float every time.

Hot-spots

At certain times all through the pike season on the Broadlands, large concentrations of pike are encountered. There are

Steve Harper is renowned for his thirty pounders. Here he slides back a fine 30lb 3oz pike.

many reasons why large numbers of pike congregate in relatively small areas of broad or river. It may be that they are following fry shoals or preparing to, or have just finished, spawning. In some cases there seems to be no apparent reason at all why the pike should behave in this way. All one can say is that the pike are there and you have to make the most of it while you can. These hot-spots may last a week, a month, a season, or even several seasons. The life of a hot-spot, however, does often seem relative to the angling pressure it receives.

Some of these hot-spots also seem to be migratory. On several waters, rivers and broads, pike seem to head for the same areas at certain times, year in, year out. This is where an angling diary comes in. It

is invaluable to see where the fish were a season or two before at the same time of the year. Once again, a picture can be built up of the pike's movements, especially on rivers, and you can try to keep one step ahead of them as the bait shoals take up their winter quarters with the pike in attendance, or when the pike search out their annual spawning grounds once again.

Broadland being flat, open and close to the sea is more affected by weather conditions than most other parts of the country. The wind is the main problem. Boats and wind just do not go together! I do not mind rain, snow, sleet, or even ice in moderation, but I would rather fish a flat calm than during gale-force winds. The pike certainly do not mind it windy, but then I have had some very good catches in flat calm conditions and have been very much more comfortable as well.

The combination of flat calm with sun-shine can kill a day's sport, but on the other hand changeable conditions with bright sunlight and clouds have been really productive. However, if we are quite honest, if we have a bait in the water, what-ever the conditions we are in with a chance. After all, it only takes one run to make a memorable season on Broadland.

THE CHALLENGE OF BROADLAND

by John Bailey
and Martyn Page

In the previous chapter Steve Harper discussed the ways in which he approaches the Norfolk Broads. Both Steve and M.P. have been members of the same specimen group in excess of a decade and have been close angling companions throughout that time. They approach the Broads, with others, as a team, sharing knowledge, fish and of course enjoyment. This approach has enabled the group to achieve consistent success throughout many years in all the Broadland waters they have fished.

We now wish to examine a few important aspects which are known to the more successful Broadland anglers, but which are often not appreciated by others. The result is that often visitors leave for home after a weekend or more in the Broadland, unsuccessful and disappointed that this 'Mecca' had not lived up to their expectations.

We must first emphasise the points contained within Steve's chapter concerning boats. There is so little accessible bank fishing on the Broads that to consider pike fishing without access to a boat would be little short of lunacy. Many Broadland anglers own, or own shares in, several boats moored at strategic positions to give maximum flexibility of venue. Believe us, the trafficking going on in boats in Broadland in the winter is unbelievable. This then is often the very first reason why the visiting angler fails. He is forced to rely on those few places where he can hire boats and hence is restricted to areas which may be overpiked and contain few of those very large fish that the area is justly famous for.

Baits and feeding

As M.P. made notes for this chapter, he sat reflecting on a complete weekend without a sign of fish. Two days before the weekend, temperatures had improved and some waters had become free of ice but the pike did not seem impressed by this change. The Sunday was spent on the Bure, a water which M.P. first fished as a young lad. His blank today was only the seventh he has experienced on that river in all those years and such was the impact created by the lack of runs, that he began muttering that all the pike, perhaps even all the fish, had died during the January freeze. Fortunately, at that time, a match angler remarked that his match had been won with a catch of three ruffe. This, although slightly reassuring M.P., did not improve the day's fishing which ended with a screaming run, which appropriately came from an underwater ice raft! More seriously, there is a lesson to be learnt: it is so often the case on the Broads that if one water is not fishing, sport is slow on the others. We have found this with very few exceptions.

If we turn to feeding times, these are not

consistent throughout different waters or indeed throughout the course of a year. It is probably true to say that there are very few Broadland waters which fish only during the evening. Most of the waters fish better during the morning, or in some cases in early afternoon and it is usual only to experience a good last hour feeding spell if there has been also a good morning feeding spell or if the pike have consistently fed throughout the day. Very rarely does one spend a day fishing on Broadland without success until that last hour arrives.

Let us examine this further. It is true to say that there is very little summer pike fishing undertaken on the Broads and their connecting rivers. Primarily this is because of the holiday boat traffic but even on the land-locked broads of the Ormesby system

few people pursue pike during the summer. We suppose this is because there are so few summer months during which to catch other species, but there is also a problem both in the amount and times during which pike seem to feed during the summer.

If we stay within the Ormesby group as a typical example, we experience two problems during these warm months. The water is excessively coloured and, secondly, there is an abundance of roach and bream in the water. A pike could lay anywhere on the broad and open its jaws but once a day to sustain itself. The roach and bream consist of all sizes so it is impossible to be selective by presenting a larger size livebait, and deadbait also seems to be less successful during this time. This could be because the pike are so widely spread.

The problems of summer piking are less

Martyn Page slides back a well-marked 27lb 7oz fish.

acute on those broads which remain crystal clear during the summer and here sport can be found during the early hours of the day and also during the latter hours. Indeed, in contrast to winter, the latter hours on these broads can, at times, prove far superior to the dawn period.

Moving into the traditional piking season, it is usual to find that throughout September to the end of November the best feeding times are during the first two or three hours of light. Progressively, as winter approaches, the later morning becomes more productive, and during the short December and January days on many waters the best sport is obtained in short consistent feeding spells throughout the day. Often the period between 10 a.m. and midday results in the most fish. As the days lengthen in the last few weeks of the season there begins a slow return to the preference for the dawn feeding spells.

We must emphasise, however, that this is a generalisation and each Broadland water seems to have its own unique key feeding time, although they all seem to fall broadly within the pattern outlined. As an example, during the last two weeks of November and the first two of December 1983, M.P. was catching fish consistently between 10 and 10.30 a.m. on a Thurne system water, and between 11.30 and 12.30 p.m. on one of the Ormesby Broads. The waters therefore conformed with the overall pattern, but the key feeding time was different on each.

A few weeks prior to that, M.P. enjoyed three consecutive sessions on different waters which produced, amongst others, twenty pound plus fish on each day, one was only two ounces under twenty-five pounds and another was in excess of twenty-six pounds. In all cases the fish came during the dawn feeding spell. This not only emphasises the changing feeding spells as winter progresses, but also is a good example of how all Broadland waters often fish well at the same time.

Leaving the question of feeding times now, the Broadland angler is also very aware of the pike's preference for different baits at different times. There is no need to cover the factors which influence the types of deadbaits used, as this is amply covered in other chapters of the book. However, there is one major factor which virtually all newcomers to Broadland seem not to appreciate. So many times M.P., for instance, has entertained anglers with a weekend on Broadland and they have left totally staggered that pike could consistently ignore their large livebaits and take, seemingly with relish, the deadbaits fished alongside.

Indeed for a livebait angler this can often prove hard to accept, but those anglers who have come to live in Norfolk soon appreciate the wisdom of these words. Indeed John Watson remarked to M.P., after two seasons' pike fishing on Broadland, that until he moved to Norfolk he would never have expected that there would be days when he could fish knowing that all his rods must be on deadbaits and that to fish a livebait rod would produce nothing but jack pike.

However, there is little need to say that this preference for deadbaits only applies on certain waters at certain times of the year. It would be totally misleading and inaccurate to suggest that you would consistently obtain results by fishing only deadbaits on the Norfolk Broads. No, of course, the truth falls somewhere in between and we would always recommend you approach these waters with an ample supply of both live and deadbaits. The point to appreciate is that at certain times of the year and for certain reasons there are periods where one will be favoured in preference to the other. Again as a generalisation, we would suggest that if you are faced with a very coloured broad during October, November and early December you will find that deadbaits are essential

Steve Harper and Dave Humphries cradle fish in the lower twenties taken from the Ormesby System. Steve's fish, on the left, is particularly beautifully marked.

and livebaits unimportant in selecting the larger fish. Later in the year as the frosts cause the water to clear and as fish also become wise to deadbaits, then live fish come into their own. Similarly in some of the more weedy broads such as those found on the Thurne system, during the months before some of the weed disappears, a deadbait can often be fished more effectively in gaps in the weed and, therefore, will often result in more fish.

There are also almost inexplicable circumstances. During a period early in 1984, a hot area produced, for M.P.'s team, two thirty pound pike, a twenty-seven and a twenty-six and several smaller twenty pound pike, all on deadbaits, and only one fish of twenty pounds on livebaits. There seemed no reason for the preference at the time and even more strangely some twelve

months later during the last few weeks of 1984, a spate of fish were caught on the same water in the same conditions, but this time all but one of the fish fell to good sized livebaits.

At first there seemed no possible explanation, but M.P. is certain now that in the second instance the fish were actually being caught amongst an abundant supply of bait fish, and in these circumstances were livebait-orientated with the good sized baits proving selective. In the first case, the area in which the fish were found was within striking distance but not amongst prey fish. The pike were resting and waiting but willing to accept the very easy meal of a dead fish lying nearby.

To summarise, the points we are making should by now be obvious. There are specific patterns to feeding times on the Norfolk waters, as indeed is true of most pike waters, and there are different periods where on certain waters the pike will take live or deadbaits in preference to the other. It is necessary to firstly appreciate both these facts and then apply them to the particular water you are fishing.

Movement and location

Steve has said much on location and mentioned pike movement. We now propose to supplement this with a discussion on some of our thoughts and experiences on the movement of pike on Broadland waters. We will first, however, mention one or two points on general location which should prove of assistance to those who do not know the Broads.

You will often find that local anglers have conflicting opinions as to where the pike on specific broads are to be found. Whereas one will tell you to cast as close to the reeds as possible or under the overhanging alder trees along the bankside, another will tell you to fish the centre, and perhaps a third will tell you to take a line twenty to thirty yards from the bank to find the fish – all on that very same water! It is unlikely that any of the three will be casting a 'red herring' as each will have been successful in the spots he recommends. Sometimes pike may be close to the reeds and at other times may wander in a seemingly aimless way across the vast expanses of open water. This is the point to be appreciated – not that a specific broad is a centre water or a reed water, but that at times it could be either. We can hardly emphasise this enough!

However, it is significant that, as boat partners, Dave Humphries and M.P. have caught twenty-five pound plus fish from seven Norfolk waters and in balance most of the Broads fish have been taken well away from the edges. Therefore for those who have not previously fished the Broads, we would suggest that you should be prepared to examine and search the open water, as opposed to always seeking sanctuary in a reedy bay. These may be more comfortable and appear more pike-looking,

but they will often not contain the fish. After all on each broad every single reedy bay or overhanging alder seems to cry out pike, but those fish cannot be everywhere at once and very often they are nowhere near those delectable reedy bays.

In order to appreciate this more fully we will now discuss the movement of pike throughout Broadland. You must first appreciate that there are two types of broads in Norfolk. The first are those connected to their supporting rivers by the means of narrow dykes, and it is these waters on which most movement can occur. However, there are also the land-locked broads and we will consider these briefly before we move on.

Obviously the points discussed in the stillwater section of this book on location and movement apply to such waters and, in particular, Vic Bellars emphasises that large stillwaters are very rarely actually still. This is so very true of the shallower Norfolk Broads where, during the times of high wind, excessive undertows can form and these undoubtedly affect pike movement. Bait fish movement also, such as the accumulation of fry in a bay in October or November, can produce hot areas for a limited time. Steve covers this point but it is also worth remembering that angling pressure will quickly destroy the hot-spot, often causing the pike to move great distances across the broad where they may then again settle in what will be for a time another hot area if we can but locate it. For much of the year though the pike seem to 'drift' from one day to the next over specific areas of the broad, requiring constant movement on the part of the angler to locate them.

On the waters where there is access to the river, it is generally accepted by Broadland anglers that a migration of fish occurs during the autumn. Roach and bream by their millions seem to leave the Broads at the first signs of winter, and make their

Dave Plummer cradles two fabulous fish of 27lb 12oz and 25lb 9oz. The head of the larger pike is a perfect pug-nosed example.

way up the rivers to the warmer more sheltered built up areas and the boat dykes. For years also, it has been accepted that the pike follow, not wishing to lose their abundant larder. This theory has, however, been questioned. Derrick Amies, for instance, puts forward the suggestion that the majority of the biggest pike do not in fact leave the Broads. Derrick has been exceedingly successful in the application of his theories, but then so too have those who maintain that the pike do in fact leave for the rivers soon after the prey fish. Who then is correct?

Both ideas probably contain an element of truth. Indeed, Vic Bellars in his discussion on the various stillwater pike types has, we feel, hit the nail on the head. Almost certainly stillwater pike can and do differ in their various characteristics. Some probably are stayers and others definitely are roamers.

Several years ago M.P. together with Dave Walls and the Anglian Water Authority, conducted a tagging programme on the River Bure to see if the theory could be proved one way or the other. Over one hundred pike were tagged and it was hoped that anglers would report the capture of tagged pike and from there proof of movement could be obtained. Some two years later there had only been two occurrences of tagged pike being reported! The first, exactly twelve months later, was caught within fifty yards of where it had originally been tagged. The conclusion that the biologists wished to adopt was that this fish had never moved. However, the second fish was reported as having been found dead during the summer on a broad several miles from where it was tagged. So then we have one fish which definitely moved and another which could well have moved and then returned the following winter to the same area, as would be expected if the movement theory applies. Could this then be a question of winter homes and summer homes? No more fish were reported but then the tags used at that time were not as efficient as those of today.

There is, therefore, very limited scientific evidence to prove any movement theory and as none of the fish tagged were large, this would not have confirmed or denied any suggestion that the larger fish stayed on the Broads. Our hunch is that some pike do stay, whereas the majority move off the Broads into the rivers. Our proof, limited although it is, lies in the results of people such as Derrick and indeed many of the Broadland anglers.

It is, however, noticeable that some time in late November results on these waters normally decline dramatically within a very short space of time, whereas suddenly sport on the rivers, and this includes results with the big fish, escalates. Later in the season, dependent on the weather, there is a similar fall in sport on the rivers. Firstly, the jacks become thankfully noticeable by their absence, followed by the bigger fish. In contrast, if one knows the spawning areas, one can soon find an increase in the number of small pike on the Broads in the latter weeks of February, and then, during the last few weeks of the season, nearby will be found the hen fish, laden with spawn.

Are these fish of the Broads the same as those of the rivers? Well, fortunately the answer is easy to obtain by careful photography and spot identification. By this approach we have established a number of cases where very large pike have been caught on the Broads in the autumn and have turned up later several miles upriver on several occasions, sometimes great distances apart, during the course of a season. Indeed, one such fish was caught by Steve Brown at twenty-six pounds fourteen ounces on a broad in the last few days of March 1983. She fell to his rod again in January 1984, but this time on the river, and weighing in excess of thirty pounds. She returned yet again for Steve on the river at the end of November 1984 weighing a few ounces more. Steve must have had that fish well trained!

So, on Broadland there definitely does appear to be a movement of many of the fish on to the river during the course of winter. Possibly some even pop back and forth between river and broad. Yet others seem to stay permanently on broads where no food fish appear to remain. Perhaps these fish feed on eels, other pike or even water-fowl. Certainly some scientific research suggests that predation of their own brethren is highest during December and January.

How then may the movement theory assist in the pursuit of large pike? Obviously it helps to know that at times of the year there is a large head of pike on the broad you wish to fish and at other times the river is the place. Results of most Broadland anglers suggest that the biggest pike are as likely, if not more so, to be found on the river in deepest winter as on the Broads. But if you know your Broads well, you will be able to find those few which remain and with a lack of food, it seems likely that they will be happy to accept a well-presented bait.

The river fish can prove more frustrating. In particular those of the Thurne can prove so nomadic that many weeks searching, even as a team, can be required in order to locate the fish. Angling pressure also soon moves the fish, and it is very rare indeed to achieve success in an area for more than two weeks before the fish move on. During the cold months of winter, with slowed metabolism, limited feeding times and the uncertainty as to whether you are fishing anywhere near a fish, searching for these big pike can unsettle the most patient angler. Perseverance will always pay dividends in the end and the rewards when the big fish are in the area can soon make the time spent trying to intercept the movement pattern become very worthwhile. When a large Broadland pike is drawn docile, defeated to the waiting net, then you cannot regret a minute of it.

A MODERN BROADLAND MASTER

Neville Fickling is certainly the most successful modern visitor to the Broadlands. Of that there is no dispute, not with a forty and four other Norfolk thirty pounders already to his credit. We met Neville on the banks of the Thurne, close to where he landed his fabulous forty-one pound pike. It was a March afternoon, mild with bursts of sunlight through the cloud. The Thurne marshlands could not have looked more beautiful: the blue sky, the golden reeds and the endless skyline from the churches to the windmills, to the sea and beyond.

There was a certain excitement in talking to a man who has become a legend. That thrill is even greater when you are with him, close to his historic battleground. Whatever happens to pike weights in the future, and both of us feel that they will continue to rise rapidly, Neville will always be remembered as the first of the modern age anglers to breach the forty pound barrier.

That afternoon there were many boats on the Thurne, indeed some of the best known pike anglers were out. Nobody had had a run. Everybody had been fishless not only today but for days previously. This is the way of the Thurne. There can be nowhere harder to tackle in the country. Blanks are the norm, you could even go so far as to say that to catch is abnormal. And yet, here is Neville with a colossal stack of big fish from the place. We asked him how he did it.

In the first place, he said, there has to be an element of luck about his fishing. Extraordinarily, he has not had a pike between twenty-five pounds and thirty pounds. They have all been under or, of course, over those weights. Others, M.P. for one, have had plenty of fish around twenty-seven or twenty-eight pounds and yet never taken a thirty pounder! Let us call it the luck of the game, or the chance factor.

But, and this is important, Neville has made the effort to get here as many times as is at all possible. He has not liked the thousands of miles of travelling, or the sleeping in cars, or leaving his wife. The cost has not been easy to find either, but he has felt it vital to fish as much or more than the locals themselves. In this way, he has kept in touch with the system, not with the angler's grapevine, but with the fish themselves. This has proved to be a vital key in his success. To sum his approach up, as he says, visitors can come to Norfolk Broadland looking just for a change of scene, for a laugh, and for a weekend away with their mates and take what comes their way. Or, they can come to do the job properly. And that means constant visits, superb baits, preparing boats and getting to know the system as intimately as any man can.

We asked Neville what he thought about the movement of pike on the system, for location here is more problematic than on any other water. So many times an angler has had one fish and thought he has stumbled on to a hot-spot, only to be disappointed and realise it was a pike passing through his swim. Not only does the system comprise miles of river, but also many hundreds of acres of featureless broad,

The Thurne winds towards the two distant Martham Broads.

much of it private or with heavily restricted entry. And, of course, there are not many pike present.

Neville agreed with what Vic Bellars has to say about the type of pike in the Large Stillwater section of this book – that there are roamers and stayers in the pike population. The roamers of the system here will always be a problem, but even the stayers will be moved on by angling pressure. There are occasional hot-spots on the system, where pike are happy to stay year in, year out – if left alone. But, if disturbed or unsettled they will leave in ones or twos or even perhaps as a large group. Neville has known fish travel eight miles from their capture point on the Fenland Drains, and the system pike can roam just as far as that.

Neville pointed out the differences between the Thurne and the Bure in this respect. The latter river has obvious holding areas and more pike. However great the pressure is on these places, there is a ready influx of new fish replacing those that have left. This is not the same on the Thurne with less definable features and a dramatically smaller head of fish. Here the scaring effect is total. Once found by anglers on the Thurne, the pike will simply disappear. It is rather like trying to hammer jelly.

M.P. in particular is interested as to why the Thurne produces bigger fish than the Bure, and we made some suggestions in the introduction to this section of the book. Neville feels the simplest answer is that ever since prymnesium, stocks have been low in the Thurne, far lower than in the Bure, and they have thrived in an environment with less competition. This is common with all species. J.B. experienced the phenomenon with the Wensum big roach boom after the disease columnaris had killed off the majority of the stocks there. All of us on the bank that afternoon are obviously concerned about the future of the Thurne. It is a small river with low stocks and the possibility of heavy fishing pressure could be critical.

Neville pointed out that in the pre-prymnesium days, angling pressure was heavy and pike mortality was immense. Gaffing, large barbed trebles and gorge techniques killed many fish. Other pike died, killed for food, for glass cases, or to be entered for fishing competitions, and yet the fishing remained excellent and there were seemingly constant replacements. He stresses that pike have a natural regulatory system and somehow impose their own control on numbers and size. Therefore, if some fish die, the back-up doubles will come through to fill the ranks of the big fish. So, providing there is a balance between mortality and recruitment Neville sees no problem.

And, of course, the Thurne fish have the added advantage of sanctuary. They do not like pressure and will leave for places that are either prohibited, or restricted, or unknown. There are tens of Broadland acres that have never seen a bait, and probably never will.

A possible problem in the recruitment theory is that Thurne big fish are probably old pike. Age seems to be related to length, and as the Thurne pike are long ones it could be that they are old ones too. Evidence from scales (which is not very reliable and largely discounted by modern research) seems to suggest that Thurne big ones are not less than fourteen years old. So, if there is a high mortality and a big fish takes a long time to come through, then Neville admitted there could be a possible upset to the natural balance.

Of interest here is Neville's present record fish of forty-nine and a half inches — as accurately as could be measured. Even for a Thurne fish this is a tremendous length as all recorded fish in the past seem to have stopped at around forty-seven inches. This length, in theory, gives a possible top weight for this fish of forty-three to forty-four pounds or even higher if variables are taken into account. There are times, for example, when it might have a four or five pound bream snugly inside it.

On a human note, Neville described his feelings on the capture of the giant fish. 'Vacant' is the word he used. He felt numbed rather than elated. At first he believed he was playing a twenty-five pound fish and not even when it was on the bank did he fully realise its size. At first he simply thought 'number five' (the fifth thirty pounder) and not until he measured it did he realise the Avon thirty-two pound scales would be useless for it. Even when he went to call for the assistance of Dave Plummer he didn't think the fish weighed more than thirty-five pounds. Only two hours or so after the needle had pointed to the forty-one pound mark, did his mind begin to race.

Very few of us will ever achieve such a feat. We will continue to catch very big fish, even enormous ones, but how does a man feel who has caught a pike which will always be a legend? Immediately, Neville saw the capture as dangerous, sapping his ambition. But as we spoke to him some three or four weeks after the capture, he knew the desire to catch was returning.

He has a very precise picture of the pike's importance to him. He has always been competitive in his fishing and wanted to do better than the others. Now he has achieved this. And yet it is not the actual landing of the fish that matters above all things. Rather, it is the jigsaw puzzle of angling that appeals to him. It is the correct assembling of all the pieces of the picture. Neville is a brilliant pike fisherman because he is intelligent and dedicated, and puts the energy that many of us dissipate in other ways into his fishing. Indeed, he puts it into pike alone. Whilst he may do a bit of carping or tenching, he is always going to be a pike man first and foremost. This is something, he says, that goes back to his childhood and now something totally a part of his nature.

Neville is happily uncomplicated when it comes to methods. All he sees are pieces to be filled in here and there, some minor improvements to be made, but there is no magical method to him, 'You can soak a herring on the bottom or off the bottom, but you just chuck it in really!' Similarly straightforward is his view on baits. Using two rods, he tends to begin with a dead on one and a live on the other and see which goes. Preferences can and do change rapidly. Pike do wise up to particular baits fished on specific methods and he gave an example of the paternostered livebait.

He did agree that there was something of a 'smelt syndrome'. Though he does not use this bait more than the others, they have landed him three of his fish over thirty pounds, including the forty. A smelt has to have something about it, he reckons. He has known the bait literally take places apart on occasions. The proviso he would make is that his smelts have always been very fresh ones. He sees this as important to success, whereas he has taken pike on herrings and mackerel that have been obscenely stale.

It was well into late afternoon. There was a general concern amongst the anglers around us that with the clearing skies, another frost would form and kill off sport the following morning. A great red sun was falling, Neville left us in his boat, away to a lonely mooring somewhere lost in the marshes.

ALWAYS BROADLAND MASTERS

Bill Giles and Reg Sandys have been famous in Broadland for a very long time. It is right that they should be so, for they are fine pike anglers and, above all, very fine men indeed. To spend an evening with them, as we did, is both pleasant and informative.

The competition that dogs so much of today's pike fishing scene is left behind in their company. They are both tolerant of all attitudes. Neither man criticises. Both men are modest. They speak of 'our' captures, and not of 'his' and 'mine'. When you leave, you realise that they both love piking in a very deep way. It is not a passion that flares and burns itself out in a few years. Both men have piked for over thirty years and neither shows the least sign of an early retirement! It is our guess that both of them will be catching twenty pound pike years hence, long after some of the present day whiz-kids have sold their gear in disillusionment.

Before you run away with the idea that the two men are relics of a bygone age, think again. J.B. has fished a certain still-water alongside both of them for some years now, and has always been roundly beaten. So have some of the distinguished guests he has had with him. Experience, watercraft and ingrained fishing lore are, J.B. has found, impossible to duplicate. In short, there are a lot of lessons many of us could learn from their attitude and their approach. Perhaps it is a dream, but it would be an excellent thing to see each and every pike angler applaud his brother, harbour no jealousy and help him to the hilt.

Bill and Reg fished through the very hectic time of pre-prymnesium Broadland. They kept their integrity. They were universally liked, then and now, and it is they who are left with the reputation. It is they who fish on while so many of their old colleagues have foundered.

In practical terms we all probably owe to Bill and Reg the pioneer work done on deadbaits. On 10 March 1950, before either J.B. or M.P. were born, Bill was spinning a dead roach. He let it drop to the bottom for some reason, and it was taken there by a pike. The following year he experimented further and found that deadbaits tended to catch the better fish. The move to sea baits was equally direct. One cold winter, roach became impossible to catch, so the two men bought some herrings, probably because they were roughly similar to roach in size, shape and colour. The broad was half an inch deep in ice and needed breaking with the boat, but they had a bonanza day. From there, they moved the method on to Ranworth Inner Broad and succeeded, so on to Heigham Sound where Peter Collins of the *Angling Times* got wind of the news. So it was that the world of piking became transformed.

We were interested in knowing if Broadland and the Thurne system in particular, were actually as good pre-prymnesium as legend now has it. Their answer was an overwhelming 'yes'. Obviously those who

Opposite *Horsey Mere — the greatest pike water in the country before prymnesium struck.*

only know the system by its modern gruelling self have no conception of what sport was once like.

Bill and Reg said that in those days they fished on average once a week. Had they known how special the fishing was, they would have gone out twice! It was a very rare weekend that they did not see a twenty pound fish come out of Horsey. Heigham was proverbial and not even that modern day graveyard, Hickling was dour. In those days they did not even need to bother much with Martham Broad. Some of the fish were huge: there was the fish that seized the seventeen pounder that Bill was playing, sulked with it across his jaws for some minutes and was never even seen from the boat. Do not forget the enormous fish that Reg hooked on a jack pike and lost by the boat in the very place that Hancock was to take his forty pounder the year afterwards.

Prymnesium came as a bombshell. The two men, all the angling world, were devastated. Frank Wright, another legendary Broadsman, rowed around the system late that summer. He reported tons of dead fish. In one area, he came upon three fish he put at over forty pounds each. Probably the best pike fishing anywhere in living history had come to an end. (The tragedy hit M.P. very hard in a different way. He had just saved up enough money to buy a scooter to get him to the system at weekends!)

Bill and Reg have their own theories about prymnesium. Just before that terrifying outbreak the River Board, as it was then, carried out extensive deep dredging around Horsey Mere and in the dykes of its catchment area. Dredging went down to a considerable depth and broke through the accumulations of centuries of silt, destroying the crust that had been formed. They believed this massive scouring of the area allowed more salt to seep into the system and the water, therefore, became more brackish and more vulnerable to the deadly algae bloom. If the gun was always cocked at the future of the system, this dredging pulled the trigger then, in the year of 1969.

They, like us, were very interested in the statistics of Neville's recent monster pike. They agreed that in the years they have known the Thurne system there had been very, very few fish of over forty-seven inches in length. Indeed, forty-seven inches they had always thought was about the natural ceiling, apart from the case possibly of the occasional freak monster.

The next day, this gave us both food for thought. Pike seem to be getting bigger. The forty pound record that has stood for so long has been surpassed at least once recently. The possibilities that we discussed seem endless. Perhaps the gradual seepage of chemicals from farmland into waters is making pike grow faster or for longer. Perhaps the new gravel pits are proving exceptional environments for big fish. Undoubtedly trout waters are producing unnaturally large pike, in the same way that protein-bombarded waters are seeing their carp population fatten.

Could we be witnessing another phenomenon of the Specimen Hunting Syndrome? At present, nearly all serious anglers are piking from October to March. This is a fact of the eighties. Perhaps new baits, new methods, and water saturation fishing is producing pike that once went unmolested. The potential of several species seems to have accelerated very quickly: tench, bream, carp and now it seems that pike too, are bursting through the ceiling of their old weights. As pike anglers, we feel that we are all entering exciting years.

Bill and Reg finished that evening by telling us of a trip to Ireland. A water was spotted. It looked superb and the two men went, mouths watering, to the local shop for a permit. The establishment, a general stores, was busy. They had to wait and as they came to be served, a queue had formed behind them. The shopkeeper wrote them out a permit, then ushered all the other customers out of the building. He shut up then and there, and took Bill and Reg to the lough for the rest of the day on a guided tour! Surely this is what being a true pike angler means. It is about helping your friends like Bill and Reg did for us that night in Bill's Norwich kitchen.

THE FINAL MEETING

On a very cold night in the closed season of 1985 some of the best known of British pike anglers gathered in an isolated country pub to discuss the book that you – and they – have just read. Each celebrity was given a brief: to comment on one particular section of the book, Broadland, the Lochs, the Rivers and the Stillwaters, and to lead a general discussion around the points that they wished to make.

Roger Miller opened the evening on the Broads. He was followed by Dave Plummer talking on the rivers. Andy Barker was third on the stillwaters and John Watson finished the evening by discussing the lochs. Barrie Rickards had undertaken to review the Fens, but work called him to Australia and we were grateful to receive his letter, reproduced at the end of this chapter. That Grand Man of piking, Vic Bellars, was present, as was the book's artist, Chris Turnbull and, of course, we two. All settled in around the fire, the curtains were drawn and we began the session around 8 p.m.

A long way past closing time, it was clear that a colossal amount of angling experience had been gathered in that room. Whatever water was mentioned, no matter how small or remote, it had been fished by one of the company. Whatever method was discussed, somebody had used it, or thought about it. The stories of big fish, new baits and strange occurrences were legion. And still, at the end of it all, the consensus of opinion was that the book is a good one and worth the writing.

On many points, the experts disagreed. We had both wanted this to at least some extent. Angling is not an exact science; there are areas of great controversy and these were quickly seized upon. Even though at times debate was intense, it was always tolerant. What would have impressed any listener was the often expressed belief that no man is always correct and that there is always room for differences of opinion and interpretation.

Broadland

Roger Miller began by questioning the need for multiplier reels that Steve Harper so stresses. He himself is quite happy with his stern drag fixed spool reels and now uses DAM SCJ with complete confidence. He went on to point out that these cost only £20 or so, compared with the £50 or more asked for a good multiplier.

The weight of the evening was against him. Andy Barker stressed that he was a relative newcomer to the boat scene and that though multipliers had taken some getting used to, he would not use anything else now when afloat. He also mentioned that multipliers were built for the heavy fifteen pound B.S. line, so often needed in boat fishing, and could accommodate many yards more than a fixed spool. John Watson called them the reels perfectly fitted for the job and said that in his experience they did everything asked of them that little bit better than the fixed spool.

We reached something of a compromise, deciding that a serious piker seeing a large part of his future fishing from a boat would be wise to invest in multipliers, but that a man contemplating just a few sessions afloat could well economise with stern drag reels. Chris Turnbull pointed out that developments in Germany are leading to reels with a memory control in the drag system which would avoid the tensioning and slackening now necessary.

An important omission in the text, so Roger thought, was a discussion on the benefits of night fishing. It is not mentioned in either the Broadland section, or in fact anywhere else in any depth. Andy said that in the Fens he has had pike until 2 a.m. on nights so cold that the grass had whitened in five degrees of frost while the river steadily iced over. He added that on big, clear stillwaters, especially those heavily fished, results have always improved at night. The period from midnight until 2 a.m. has been particularly productive.

This latter observation led us into a discussion on the development of piking in general. Andy remembered that as the angling pressure on Hollowell reservoir built up, the pike became wary to the point of giving twitch bites only. No full bodied runs developed, only a gentle tightening and slackening of the line. He did believe it possible that better results could have come at night when the pike would feel less vulnerable. Roger and J.B. both felt that pike have long been underestimated and that their ability to recognise dangerous baits and methods is well developed.

The mood of the meeting was that whilst pike are probably not quite as quick to learn as are carp, there are similarities between the two species and special baits, night fished, could become important on some waters probably well into the future.

Rivers

Dave Plummer felt it worth stressing that many river systems are very quick to flood and to become out of sorts. He was referring particularly to his native rivers and the frustration he often felt after travelling seventy miles or more only to find them unfishable. He reinforced the importance of snags to river pike, agreeing that typical barbel and chub haunts often held the big predators too.

Dave picked up the spirit of the chapters well. He liked Mick Brown's 'gusto' and obvious enjoyment in what he does on the rivers and his pleasure in any good fish, not necessarily just twenty pounders. As he said, Mick's piece really makes any man want to get at river pike. Equally, he had a lot of praise for Bob Mousley's determination to do well at all costs, or certainly at the sacrifice of fishing with friends. Dave calls Bob a realist, a man who would not tolerate restrictions and therefore fishes alone. Neither attitude is wrong. John Watson summed it up by saying a man's attitude is his own.

We all agreed that river piking is underrated, that there are probably hundreds of miles of unexplored river in this country, and that a twenty pound pike, marvellous anywhere, is an especial triumph from a river.

Dave stressed the difference in water types and that some rivers are capable of bigger fish than others. M.P. mentioned that Bob Mousley's network of rivers had just been producing fish of over twenty-five pounds, which are huge by any standards.

Dave finally said, as an afterthought almost, that he is not too keen on freezing days for river piking. Still on weather, Andy said that in high water conditions, he has found river pike often only inches, not feet, from the bank. His belief is that they are escaping the main push there. M.P. questioned this by saying that in the strong moving tidal Waveney, the big fish were often well from the bank. Andy countered by asking what the water was actually doing underneath the surface in these places, and suggested that the fish could have found mid-river snags to shelter behind to escape the full water force.

Big stillwaters

Referring to Eddie Turner and Bill Hancock's section on drifting, Andy Barker commented unfavourably on the paragraph suggesting trout livebaits as possible substitutes for indigenous fish. He did point out that livebaiting, anyway, is a sensitive issue and that transporting trout for baits is illegal. Dave agreed here. We stressed that Eddie and Bill did not move trout around and that we ourselves had suggested the possibility.

Roger and John believed the offending paragraphs should be left in, if only to force pikers to think about the subject. Roger said that using native fish is also detrimental to stocks and, therefore, conservationally to be discouraged. Perhaps we would say that trout should only be used *if* allowed, and that pikers should not use livebaits that are desired by matchmen or pleasure anglers. Everyone in the room agreed that livebaiting is an essential method, but that we must protect our image and do as little harm as possible.

Andy saw drifting as only one method in the angler's repertoire and here we all agreed. Any reader should not think drifting will answer *all* stillwater problems. Conditions do have to be sympathetic. Andy even suggested it will be a phase only, and does not see drifting as the dawn of a new thinking, experimenting era. We tended to disagree. Eddie Turner's designs and ideas, we feel, will go from strength to strength.

Moving on to Paul Snepp's generally agreed excellent piece, Andy did mention that jacks fished dead are also very efficient. He also said that whilst they are good for very big fish, on 'hammered' waters they are useful as a change bait for average sized doubles. On some of Andy's waters, anglers even row dead jacks to the areas they want to fish.

Andy stressed that using jacks is a con-troversial issue once again, and Dave suggested that it was hypocritical for the Pike Anglers' Club and for leading pikers to campaign to put pike back if they are then to use their young as bait. John said that he personally could never use a jack as bait on principle, but again felt it was up to the individual's conscience. We would add that there is no biological evidence that removing some jacks upsets the pike balance or spoils future pike fishing. In fact, this is probably improved, as the competition for food is thereby much reduced.

Turning to Vic Bellar's lengthy chapter, we all agreed that he had provided a great deal of factual depth to the book. It is a reference chapter as much as anything which can be used quite like a text book.

Vic goes into great detail on echo sounders and graph recorders and we asked those present for a quick synopsis of their views on them. Andy regarded them as electronic plummets, as aids, as the modern approach to making things easier for ourselves. Chris suggested that their use on familiar waters would fill in the closed season instructively, and M.P. saw them as a teaching aid, as an extension of our interest and knowledge. John Watson agreed, but did feel that they are not ethical as a fish finding device (some of the graph recorders actually print individual fish on their screens). Vic simply stated that they are the coming trend and that electronic gadgetry will not be resisted.

Lochs and loughs

The night was getting on: the landlord had the glint of last orders in his eyes, and his wife had brought out a magnificent platter of sandwiches which had disappeared before the hungry heroes. We moved into the final section.

John Watson emphasised the importance of the pre-dawn period on Lomond and of sticking to the same loch (which does form the basis of Gord Burton and Frank Pennington's experience), and discussed the powan stocks. He stressed that much is made of the powan as a staple food for pike and that they are very difficult to obtain as bait.

Overall, John was sceptical about the varying attractions of silver scaled fish, perch and 'dark' fish like crucian carp. His hunch was to say that outstanding captures on any of these species were flukes and that patterns are not easily drawn. Obviously, the controversy between the supporters of 'silver' and of 'dark' baits on Lomond is an old one. John personally sees big pike preference as something of a lottery.

He moved on to say that it is possible to bank fish Lomond and some other lochs, even though Gord and Frank restrict their piece to boatfishing. Many English anglers travel North at spawning time, camp around a shallow bay for anything up to a month and wait for waves of spawning fish to move in. Andy added that a similar tactic is used on Irish loughs. We all agreed that such methods were limited and were not at all part of the true big water scene. Fish can be caught, some of them large ones, but the water has not been fully read or 'cracked'. The achievement is not what Gord and Frank were describing.

Andy thought it important that the difference between Lomond and the other lochs be emphasised. The former is far richer than most other Scottish waters and Awe, in particular, is comparatively barren of fish.

John did say that though he has fished Lomond many times, the chapter still fired him, made him want to get back across the border. Indeed, the piece was composed by men who write as they feel, and by men who love fishing intensely. The same thing, John said, is true of George Higgins' inspirational chapter. Here too, he felt with the anglers, watching the nodding rod tips

and the tail walking pike. We all liked the vision of two or three men trolling in a boat, happy in each others success.

So, we moved to the last controversy of the night. John raised the question of George's trolled deadbait hooking rig that was described and drawn in the text. We all debated that very fundamental question of how a pike gets hooked. Much depends on the range being fished and the bait being used, but there are three possible alternatives: the pike hooks itself, the hooks are struck from the bait into the pike, or thirdly, the pressure is simply maintained on the fish so that the opportunity to shake the bait free is not presented. In the end, we decided that all three solutions fit respective occasions. Andy has seen pike throw baits clear and then hook themselves on the free falling trebles. Vic obviously felt that with his rigs and tandems, the strike pulls the hooks clear of the bait and into the pike. J.B. knew that once the pressure was relaxed on his thirty six pound fish in the net, the hooks simply fell clear.

So, right at the end, the message of the evening was maintained. In this game, you cannot be dogmatic. One man's piking must never be another man's poison.

The evening closed and even in the frosted car park last minute conversations took place here and there, in ones and twos. The book, the Broads, the rivers, the lochs, the reservoirs and essentially the pike – our minds buzzed with it all and we could have gladly talked on until the dawn.

Barrie Rickards' letter on the Fens

Dear John and Martyn,

I greatly enjoyed the two sections on Fenland piking. I appreciate that the articles are not intended to be all-embracing and will, therefore, confine my own remarks to the points raised and to related matters.

Keith Mottram is confident that deadbaits 'will give him the results'. What results? If he means results to his satisfaction, then I support him, but if he means as good as livebaits then I do not. No matter how tiny and tatty the Fenland drain, no matter how shallow and weedy, I find that livebaits give you more fish, and plenty of big ones, though naturally the average weight is less. I wish this were not so, because I have a firm preference for deadbaiting – I just enjoy the simplicity of bait gathering, transport and fishing techniques. Of course you cannot – or should not – make a comparison if you only use one method. Over a long period of time livebait comes out distinctly better.

We would re-affirm that Keith Mottram used deadbaits solely as there was a livebait ban on the water.

Perhaps this is an appropriate point to discuss, briefly, barometric pressure. Members of the P.A.C. have been providing Tim Cole and me with their active versus static run results, and I have been carefully noting my runs, relative to obtaining pressure, during 1983 and 1984. If anything it supports even more strongly than before:

1 That if the pressure goes low and stays low for two days or more, then if the fish feed at all it tends to be on static deadbaits.

2 That when the pressure rises the fish become generally more active and will often ignore deadbaits, fished static, altogether. Of course, there are exceptions, but surprisingly few. When the pressure is high there is a tendency for pike to take anything, and on shallowish waters this can include static, bottom fished deadbaits, as well as livebaits, lures and wobbled baits.

Hot-spots can, in fact, be fished for several years without destroying them. I am currently fishing one that has survived seven years. The point is that I am the only angler fishing it. Overfishing *does* destroy hot-spots – whether the fish die, learn, or move, hardly matters from the angler's seat. At least not as far as immediate results go.

Mind you, I do not really think Keith Mottram is talking about hot-spots in the way I originally defined them. All three of his examples do have features, as he so rightly says, but in the absence of comparative results from adjacent swims over a period of time, it is hard to decide whether his hot-spots are merely good holding areas, transient hot-spots (see my book, *Fishing for Big Pike*) or genuine hot-spots. Clearly they are worth fishing, whatever!

And I do assure you that many Fenland hot-spots have no features whatsoever (unless one counts the odd half brick on the bottom). Nor am I convinced that roach shoals are related to pike hot-spots. Pike do follow shoals, of course, but I am certain that pike of a size have a communal lair to which they return when not actively hunting; and roach do not often frequent such places – just as you and I would not normally stroll through the home lair of a pride of lions which, incidentally, also hunt far and wide and then return to their pad. If you put a dredger through some of my hot-spots you would not notice much difference! So I do not think Keith 'rather explodes' the 'phantom' hot-spot idea at all. They exist.

I certainly applaud the thinking approach – or, rather, the try anything approach – of Dennis Smith and Tony Lovell. I have not found it necessary to ring the changes quite so often as it seems they do, although clearly this can do no harm. I found some years ago that a polystyrened bait worked really well one day, but the next day they wanted it hard on the bottom again, and vice versa. It is easy to move on to something new after a couple of bad days when all it means, or may mean, is that the pike really were off the feed or on livebaits when all you had was dead. I wonder if they have tried coloured livebaits: it is very effective and the colour wears off in twenty four hours or so and the golden roach reverts to his true self!

I hope I have not seemed too critical in my remarks: naturally I have confined myself to bits I disagree slightly with or otherwise feel I have a contribution to make.

Finally, it remains only to take mild issue with John and Martyn on the introduction to this section. If by the decline of the Fens you mean *general* decline – bream, roach, etc. – then I am not fully qualified to argue with you, except to say that in the drains without zander the bottom fishing has remained quite superb throughout. Those who trot out that there are several factors affecting the Fenland decline, really should read carefully what Neville Fickling and I wrote in *Zander*, or what Ron Linfield and I said in the Institute of Fisheries Management journal. All other variables are merely those that are with us, on and off, most of the time. Fenland piking, however, is a subject I do know something about, and I know that whereas some very popular stretches were hammered to death (and hence declined for that reason alone), most of the Fens has remained good piking and with good fish. My own results have hardly changed except, perhaps, to get slightly better.

Barrie Rickards

AUTHORS AND CONTRIBUTORS

The contributors to this book represent some of the very best anglers in the British Isles at this moment in time. We think that you, the reader, will find these short pen portraits interesting for many reasons. You will see that they are highly individual men, often with strong opinions, often differing amongst themselves. For instance, Bob Mousley does not care for best fish lists and yet the majority obviously like to illustrate the depth and breadth of their experience.

You will notice that nearly all of these men began fishing in their very early childhood. This means that they have worked up the hard way, and that their knowledge in all cases is profound, learnt from thousands of sessions on the waterside. There are no 'instant experts' here, just hundreds and hundreds of years of fishing experience. You will also see that probably because of this, almost all say how deeply involved they are in the countryside and natural world. Angling is central to all their lives. They care passionately about the whole waterside environment and represent a very positive conservationist force there.

John Bailey

I have been fishing for just on thirty years and have caught just about every freshwater species that swims. Now, if there is a challenge or excitement in it I am happy to go for anything from salmon to dace and even tried recently to break the gudgeon record!

Over the years I have built up a big fish list which includes several hundred two pound plus roach to over three pounds, rudd of over three pounds, carp and pike into the mid-thirties, and double figure barbel and bream.

I have written for the angling and wildlife press for twelve years and am the author of two recent books, *In Visible Waters* and *Travels with a Two Piece*.

I am not a lover of the 'big fish scene', of the merry-go-round of current 'in' waters, and much prefer to hunt less well-known fish. This desire for seclusion is because my love for angling is firmly embedded in a feeling for nature and unspoilt environments. I am increasingly content to catch very few fish each season, only looking for those that spell some new excitement. I will no longer disturb fish just for the sake of it, there has to be some larger purpose behind it.

My immediate projects include expeditions after very large sea trout, big lake trout, small river salmon, creek mullet and estate lake carp. In fact, angling is an ever unfolding adventure story of which I will never tire and never be able to write the final chapter.

Martyn Page

Having spent many years in search of larger size fish and having caught my statutory quota of twenty pound plus pike, double figure barbel and seven pound tench, increasingly I look for different ventures. I harbour the desire for an American or Canadian musky, a big Irish pike, or even an Amur from Russia. Other unusual species also, such as catfish or the Mahseer occupy my mind. This is where in future years I expect to broaden my angling horizons but at the same time my week to week angling will still rely on the enjoyment of capturing a large fish, whatever the species, in good company.

This is particularly the case with pike, where I have seen an increase in the bitter ultra-cult competition, which gave the carp scene its bad name during the seventies, creep into pike angling. Angling is for pleasure and my greatest concern is for the pointless bickering and backbiting still present in piking circles today. Whether it is through jealousy or any other reason it can only do harm to pike angling and to the whole sport. I myself find no greater pleasure than fishing with good friends and other pike anglers. Of course, I like to be successful but for me, now, this is certainly not the most important consideration.

Of ambitions, I have few. I did have an ambition of capturing a pike in every pound class up to my biggest but this has been fulfilled this year. I would like one day to capture a larger pike, say a twenty nine or perhaps a thirty, and if it is several pounds heavier then my ambition of filling in the gaps will return. I also like to capture at least one fish over twenty five pounds per year, but if I failed during one year that would not matter greatly.

I have one other strong feeling in angling and that is that all anglers who spend some time taking something from the sport should put something back. The last four years I have been Treasurer, and of late both Treasurer and Secretary, of the Pike Anglers' Club, and by my work for this club I hope that I at least can be said to have contributed my share. Even so as I hand over my duties, during the course of this year I still intend to contribute not only to the Pike Anglers' Club, but also in other ways to angling. I am sure that if every angler made an effort to do likewise, we could all become more united with the result that we would protect our present fishing, create more new fishing and certainly never bow to any threats by, say, the misguided anti-angling organisations. With a united front angling could show the media that without us the country's waters would be polluted and lacking in the very fish that the 'antis' seem so keen to protect. It is anglers who protect the country's waters and the fish therein but it is also anglers who do nothing to protect their rights!

Finally, what do I see as the future for pike angling? Certainly increased competition will lead to problems, especially if people are allowed to fish for pike without guidance. If I were an extremist I would recommend compulsory membership of the P.A.C. for all pike anglers, however, an extremist I am not. But something will need to be done and therefore to all readers, I strongly recommend that your contribution to angling should be membership of the P.A.C. and the A.C.A. and the guidance of new anglers when seen on the banks. In this way better handling of our pike will be encouraged, which will go a long way towards helping conserve both our pike fishing and that of our children.

Andy Barker

His entry into the big fish scene was with the Coventry Circus Group in the early 1970s when he and his friends pioneered many of today's methods. For example, Andy developed a forerunner of the drifting float.

Andy is an angler of colossal experience and knowledge who has fished countless waters throughout Britain. Whatever he now says has to command respect.

Within a few years, he has built up one of the country's leading tackle businesses, founded on knowing what specialist anglers require and at what price they can afford it.

Vic Bellars

According to his mother, Vic started, or perhaps attempted to start, an angling career when he was four years old. Missing from his home in King's Lynn he was eventually discovered sitting on the quayside, after a frantic search involving the police. Legs dangling and dunking a whole raw potato connected to a length of string by a hairpin, he was understood to have informed his 'captors' that he was fishing and wanted to be left alone!

After a career in the Navy in both peace and war, and in spite of a wide variety of other interests, fishing has always been an abiding passion which after fifty years shows no sign of diminishing. Vic is an honorary member of the Leighton and District Specimen Group and a member of the Norwich based Broadland Group. He serves on the Norfolk and Suffolk Consultative Committee, attends the National Federation of Anglers Eastern Region meetings and is a delegate to the Birmingham Anglers' Association. He was for four years President of the Pike Anglers' Club of Great Britain.

Vic aptly styles himself a pleasure fisherman for he fishes for enjoyment. He is entirely uncompetitive with no interest whatsoever in amassing impressive totals of twenties, and has never bothered to chase around the country fishing the 'in' waters. Vic normally fishes waters within easy reach of his home.

Edward Hewitt, an American angler, once wrote of the phases that a fisherman passes through in his lifetime. First, he wants to catch the most fish, then he is only interested in catching the largest, and finally he wishes to catch the most difficult regardless of size. Vic Bellars says that he now fits well and truly into the last category.

Mick Brown

Mick, at thirty-eight, is married with two small children. He has spent most of his working life as an engineer in the plastics industry.

He enjoys fishing for most species but specialises in the predators, especially pike. His best pike is twenty-six pounds six ounces and he concentrates on river fish. He has taken over two hundred fast water doubles and twenties from four different rivers. His best fish list includes eight double figure zander to thirteen pounds three ounces, eels to five pounds eleven ounces, carp to twenty-two pounds twelve ounces and chub to five pounds three ounces. He says his most memorable moment in fishing was watching two twenty pound plus pike take his bait from under the rod tip on consecutive casts.

He hates to see fish badly handled or in any way maltreated and in particular, he is disillusioned by the carnage carried out amongst pike by the salmon anglers on the Severn and Wye. He calls on all true pikers to defend the sport in every possible way, at the very least by joining the P.A.C. He himself has rescued hundreds of pike from certain death and found new homes for them, oblivious to the time and the cost this has meant to him.

Gord Burton and Frank Pennington

Gord is the better known, extrovert half of this team in which Frank keeps a relatively low profile. Both men are considered as leaders of the current generation of Lomond anglers and both have many fine pike to their credit. Both men have a great love for the big Scottish waters and their enthusiasm is infectious. Indeed, on one occasion Gord kept a P.A.C. audience spellbound for over two and a half hours talking about his life on Lomond.

Both men were fired by Richard Walker's inspirational articles on big Lomond fish and began to travel regularly north of the border from the late 1970s. They have had many loch twenties and believe passionately in the existence of Lomond monsters. For both Gord and Frank, their ultimate aim is a Lomond forty!

Neville Fickling

Neville has landed well over a hundred twenty pounders in an angling career dedicated to the pursuit of big pike. We consider his recent record just reward for the lifetime of effort he has spent.

He is presently Membership Secretary of the National Association of Specialist Anglers, an organisation in which his wife Kathy also plays a leading role. It is largely thanks to the both of them that recent N.A.S.A. conferences have become such a success and such a feature of the British closed season.

Neville is a trained fishery biologist and he has researched deeply into the lives and habits of pike and zander.

Bill Giles and Reg Sandys

The two men began fishing together in the early 1950s, which must make them the longest standing team in piking. They say they never get on each others' nerves and take it strictly in turns to pick new swims in the course of the day. They share in each others' successes totally and have taken eighty-one twenty pound plus fish in their career together, capped by Reg's thirty pound gravel pit fish.

Their ambition is to continue piking together for as long as possible and while they do so, we feel there will always be at least one boat where sanity and moderation remain.

Steve Harper

Stephen Harper is married with two children and is a commercial artist by profession. He lives on the outskirts of Norwich with the River Wensum within casting range from his garden.

He started fishing at the age of six, and since then, has taken specimens of most of Britain's freshwater species. Main interests include pike (best thirty-two pounds nine ounces), zander (best thirteen pounds eleven ounces) and barbel (best eleven pounds fourteen ounces). The latter fish is noteworthy in that it was the first double figure barbel to be caught from Norfolk.

His main ambition is simply to enjoy fishing but would also like to get his name into Fred Buller's *Domesday Book*!

George Higgins

George Higgins has served apprenticeship on all Ireland's species in his time and what he has achieved in piking, which is a great deal, he generously says he owes to his friends Roy Smyth and Alex Dickey. It was they who first took him trolling and showed him how rich a pikeman's world can be. To date he has caught 2,341 pike and at least fifty over twenty pounds. A twenty-four pounder in 1959 was his first big one.

George has a very deep love for both his sport and his country. He writes, 'I love the freedom afloat, amid the magic and miles of Ireland, where the wind and rain are endured and the finest days are treasured. Every new day is a bonus to the living, and every pike I catch a bonus to me. I can ask for no more, nor expect better.'

Roger Miller

Roger, twenty-six, is Suffolk born, now a Norfolk policeman. He says that he was lucky in his formative years as many friends of his farming family allowed him to fish exclusive Suffolk pools for carp and rudd.

He was in his teens when he decided to hunt big fish in earnest and now his bests include chub to five pounds eight ounces, roach to two pounds fifteen ounces, barbel to ten pounds two ounces, tench to seven pounds eight ounces, bream to nine pounds six ounces, and rudd to two pounds thirteen ounces. Pike are probably his first love and he has many twenties to his credit up to twenty-four pounds thirteen ounces.

He believes that there is a lot to be optimistic about in the current specialist fishing scene. He detects a strong feeling of unity amongst anglers and a growing brotherhood throughout the sport.

Keith Mottram

Keith is thirty-four, a self employed builder and, like so many of our contributors, has been fishing since he was a boy.

Pike are now his major quarry and he has taken them to twenty-five pounds and four ounces. Other good fish include barbel to seven pounds five ounces, trout, tench and chub. He puts long hours into his fishing and believes it is vital to work for results. His periods on the drains are made much more pleasant by his dedication to the countryside and his interest in wildlife.

Bob Mousley

Bob is a refreshing angler in today's scene. He is happy searching out any species of fish, providing he has a chance of good ones, so he calls himself the 'multi-specialist angler'. Nor does he like best fish lists which, after all, do nothing but for the ego.

Most of all we like his realistic ambitions. We quote from his letter:

'Most dedicated specimen fish enthusiasts have secret aims. I have fished almost since birth and have specialised from the age of twelve. In all that time not one target weight has been achieved. Or, then again, has it? When I reach one goal my sights automatically set themselves higher. Thinking back to when I was a lad, my dreams were of twenty pound pike and two pound roach. Now, they are of thirty pounds and three pounds, and so with other fish. Anglers say it is better to travel than to arrive. In my case I keep extending the distance, always enjoying the journey. A few days after writing this, I caught a roach at three pounds one ounce. Is that fate perhaps?'

Dave Plummer

He was a Yorkshire train driver, derailed to Norfolk where he is now developing a tackle business in Norwich. He is one of the country's leading specialist anglers with a staggering big fish list of pike to over thirty pounds, barbel over thirteen pounds, tench over eight pounds and bream of over eleven pounds, plus many other large carp, roach and rudd.

He has been criticised, unfairly we think, for his intense attitude to the sport. Much nearer the truth is that Dave has an unquenchable love for fishing and the waterside.

Barrie Rickards

Barrie is one of the most well liked and respected specialist anglers of the modern era. He is the inspiration to many of today's pike anglers. He is also one of the country's leading authorities on pike behaviour in the UK.

He was one of the founders of the P.A.C., taking over and revitalising the near extinct Pike Society. He went on to be Secretary of the organisation for the first four years of its life. He is currently engaged in important work for all anglers in preparing guidelines and fact sheets that we can use to answer the charges of the 'antis'.

Barrie is the most famous living pike angler with fish of over thirty pounds in his career. He is renowned for his Fenland captures in the 1960s and 1970s and for his co-authorship of the revolutionary book, *Fishing for Big Pike*, published now fourteen years ago.

Dennis Smith and Tony Lovell

Both Dennis and Tony say that they were greatly influenced in their early pike fishing days by the writings of such legendary heroes as Fred Wagstaffe and Bob Reynolds. It was the exploits of these latter fisherman that introduced them to the pleasures of lure fishing and, in particular, trolling, which they find one of the most demanding and exciting forms of pike fishing. The pair are, of course, phenomenally successful on the Fens and here they give much of the credit to Barrie Rickards and Ray Webb, who both pioneered so much modern thinking.

The decline of individual drains pushed Dennis and Tony more to the gravel pits of their area, and they praise Martin Gay's ideas and writings for the sound basis they used to experiment from.

Lastly, we love the confidence of this marvellous pair of anglers. They generally take with them upwards of two stone of bait for those exceptional days when the pike go wild. J.B. comments that on occasion they have probably had more doubles in a day than he has seen in his life!

Paul Snepp

My first large pike was netted about fifteen years ago and remains a highlight in thirty

odd years of involvement with angling. I have long been fascinated with pike and their habits and realise that they are not the mindless brutes so many consider them to be. Yet they are only a speck in a fishing universe so vast that I feel pulled, pushed and beguiled by countless species and habitats, I hardly know where to let my attention rest next.

Angling crosses all social and international boundaries. It permits the body and the mind to wander to so many wondrous places and encounter marvellous characters from all walks of life. Immortality would be a priceless asset in allowing us to simply scratch the surface. Regrettably, not all mankind has our appreciation. Our protective vigilance must never cease.

Chris Turnbull

Chris began fishing as an eleven year old and is now probably the country's leading fish artist. He is a genuine all round angler with pike to twenty-seven pounds fourteen ounces, carp to twenty-seven pounds eight ounces and tench to eight pounds. His great ambition is to catch a thirty-five pound plus pike and to see all anglers treat the watersides of Britain with greater respect.

He is a member of the Anglian Water Fisheries Consultative Committee and would dearly like to see the introduction of catfish into more stillwaters.

Eddie Turner and Bill Hancock

Both men come from the Lea Valley, an area of intense piking competition. This has bred in them a mobile, thinking approach.

They are predominantly livebait anglers and as a team have landed many twenty five pound plus pike from every imaginable environment (and indeed as we write, the pair are piking in Ireland).

Recently, they have begun to market the tackle innovations which they have used with such great success in the past and already they are beginning to make significant changes to the British pike fishing scene.

John Watson

John is an intensely enthusiastic angler. He comes from Lancashire which is a relatively sparse coarse fishing county and, perhaps, this background has bred in him a burning desire to succeed.

He burst to fame as an eel angler and is now a highly respected all rounder, but in latter years he has specialised to some extent with pike, taking several thirties and many twenty pounders. His love of predators spreads naturally to the zander and he has had specimens to over thirteen pounds.

John was Secretary of the P.A.C. to which post he brought his drive and energy for two and a half years. His strong, widely publicised beliefs on fish handling and unhooking has probably saved the lives of thousands of pike during the last few seasons.

OTHER FISHING BOOKS PUBLISHED BY THE CROWOOD PRESS

Travels with a Two Piece by John Bailey

A collection of writing inspired by the author's journeys along the rivers of England with an ancient two piece fly fishing rod. Beautifully illustrated by Chris Turnbull.
Illustrated with line drawings.
160 pages. 220×160mm. Hardback. £9.95.

River Fishing by Len Head

Len Head explains how to read waters and set about catching the major coarse fishing species. Sections on habitat and behaviour, baits, tackle and techniques.
Illustrated with colour and b&w photographs and diagrams.
128 pages. 234×156mm. Hardback. £7.95.

Boat Fishing by Mike Millman, Richard Stapley and John Holden

A concise but detailed guide to modern boat fishing. Includes discussion on tackle, fish behaviour, baits, fishing on the drift, reef and sandbank fishing, dinghies, wrecking, and boat casting.
Illustrated with colour and b&w photographs and diagrams.
120 pages. 234×156mm. Hardback. £7.95.

Stillwater Coarse Fishing by Melvyn Russ

A guide to the maze of tackle, baits, tactics and techniques that surround the cream of coarse fishing in Britain.
Illustrated by colour and b&w photographs and diagrams.
120 pages. 234×156mm. Hardback. £7.95.

In Visible Waters by John Bailey

In this beautifully illustrated book John Bailey reveals the deep insight that he has gained over nearly thirty years closely observing the lives of the coarse fishing species.
Illustrated with colour and line drawings.
156 pages. 245×180mm. Hardback. £9.95.

Imitations of the Trout's World by Bob Church and Peter Gathercole

This book describes advanced fly tying techniques not widely known and, with the use of superb colour photography, explores the link between the natural and the artificial. The reader is also taken on a guided tour of major waters in the British Isles where local methods and practical tips are revealed.
Illustrated with colour and b&w photographs and diagrams.
176 pages. 270×210mm. Hardback. £12.50.

Long Distance Casting by John Holden

A guide to tackle and techniques of long-range casting in saltwater, including sections on reel modifications, advanced rods and pendulum casting.
Illustrated with b&w photographs and diagrams.
96 pages. 297×210mm. Hardback. £8.95.

The Beach Fisherman's Tackle Guide by John Holden

Covers rods, reels, accessories, rigs and maintenance, with good illustrations and photographs on subjects from tying knots to building rods.
Illustrated with b&w photographs and diagrams.
122 pages. 297×210mm. Hardback. £8.95.

An Introduction to Reservoir Trout Fishing
by Alan Pearson

Tackle, casting, flies, bank and boat fishing and where to fish are a few of the topics covered in this useful beginner's guide.
Illustrated with b&w and colour photographs and diagrams.
136 pages. 210×130mm. Hardback. £5.95.

Rods and Rod Building by Len Head

A manual of rod building which also offers detailed guidance on design and the selection of rods for all major branches of fresh and saltwater fishing.
Illustrated with colour and b&w photographs and diagrams.
96 pages. 235×165mm. Hardback. £6.95.

Books listed above are available through booksellers but, in case of difficulty, they can be ordered direct (enclosing cost of books plus 10% for postage and packing) from:
The Crowood Press, Ramsbury, Wiltshire SN8 2HE, England

Details listed above are correct at the time of going to press but are subject to alteration without prior notice.